CW00553562

'CHHE – SAAT'

Memoir of an Officer of the
6th/7th Rajput Regiment

'CHHE – SAAT'

Memoir of an Officer of the 6th/7th Rajput Regiment

STUART OTTOWELL

MANOHAR
2008

First published 2008

© Stuart Ottowell, 2008

ISBN 81-7304-763-4

Published by
Ajay Kumar Jain *for*
Manohar Publishers & Distributors
4753/23 Ansari Road, Daryaganj
New Delhi 110 002

Typeset by
Kohli Print
Delhi 110 051

Printed at
Lordson Publishers Pvt. Ltd.
Delhi 110 007

In memory of my beloved wife
Shirley

Contents

Illustrations

MAPS

Foreword

Kohima, Imphal and Meiktila are the names of hard fought battles during the Burma Campaign of the Second World War. To commemorate the performance of Indian troops in these battles, the Gentlemen Cadet companies of the Indian Military Academy at Dehradun are named after these: Alamein in North Africa, Cassino and Sangro in Italy, and post-independence Naushera and Zojila are also thus honoured and preserved. As a Gentlemen Cadet I had the honour to have been in Meiktila Company for two years before being commissioned into the Rajput Regiment in June 1956. Later, as I settled down in the service, my interest in military history was stimulated by talking to regimental veterans of many of the famous actions of the Second World War in North Africa and Burma. Three of our famous old battalions, the 1st, 2nd and 4th were present in Burma. Of the war raised battalions, the 6th earned four battle honours in a row: 'Capture of Meiktila', 'Meiktila', 'Defence of Meiktila' and 'Rangoon Road' which spoke of an unusual and outstanding performance.

Stuart Ottowell's *'Chhe – Saat'* provides a first hand account of how this newly formed infantry battalion, led by a remarkable Commanding Officer and an innovative bunch of officers, VCOs (JCOs) and NCOs – which included the author, could quickly adapt to operating with armour with great élan and flexibility in and around Meiktila. Stuart Ottowell's narration is remarkable as it focuses on events that occurred more than sixty years ago. Veterans of the 'Burma Star' generation, now in their eighties, can again relive some of the events of those far off days.

The Japanese had overrun the whole of Burma, but the battles of Kohima and Imphal were bitterly contested and proved to be the turning point for the campaign. After these battles the 14th Army under General Bill Slim seized the initiative and went on to the offensive. While IV Corps threatened Mandalay, the secret build up to the south by 33 Corps led to the strategic masterstroke, an attack across the Irrawaddy to capture Meiktila. 17 Indian Infantry Division – the 'Black Cat' formation – was in the forefront and after the initial success also absorbed the violent Japanese reactions. The fighting around Meiktila broke the Japanese organized defences and made it possible to proceed faster on the road to Rangoon. *'Chhe – Saat'* narrates some of events at the cutting edge.

The 6th Battalion of the 7th Rajput Regiment (hence the name of the book – *'Chhe – Saat'*) was raised in 1940 and demobilized and disbanded, after the war ended, at the Regimental Centre at Fatehgarh. Well after Independence, following the disastrous war with China, the present day 6th Battalion (Meiktila) of the Rajput Regiment was re-raised in 1963. The practice of numbering Indian infantry regiments preceding the war was discontinued and the suffix of '7th' was dropped in 1945. The existing 6th Battalion took an active part in the Indo-Pak war of 1965 in the Kashmir Valley, and later in the war for the liberation of Bangladesh in 1971 in the Sylhet Sector.

Field Marshal K.M. Cariappa, OBE, was the first Colonel of the Rajput Regiment from 1947 to 1957. Later, I was the sixth Colonel of the Regiment from 1987 to 1991. I feel honoured that I have been asked to write this Foreword as a brief introduction to *'Chhe – Saat'*. This is a most readable book.

Major General (Retired)
Ashok Kalyan Verma, AVSM
The Rajput Regiment

Preface

The War Years, 1939–45, were times of vast upheaval, danger and death. It was a time when outrageous risks were taken by the main protagonists in the hope of winning the war – nations were on the march, the powerful oppressed the weak – allegiances and loyalties were changed at the drop of a hat.

Throughout this time the Indian Army stood firm and the 7th Rajput Regiment, one of the most senior regiments, having been raised in 1778, was there to play its part in the defence of the subcontinent, in Burma and also in the Middle East.

In all theatres of war generals and their armies were trying to build on whatever localized success had been achieved, but the Germans and then the Japanese found out to their cost that units of the Indian Army were not only resilient but capable of responding in kind and finally securing complete defeat of the enemy.

This document records my personal remembrances, experiences and recollections of my service with the 'Dashing Sixth' from 1942 to 1945. It endeavours to touch on the life and times we all lived through during those tumultuous years. I was immensely privileged and honoured to be a part of the 6th Battalion at that time. The 6th Battalion was raised, however, as a result of war and thus sadly, in this incarnation never really saw peacetime soldiering in pre- and post-war India.

I have been able to draw freely on the personal War Diary of Colonel E.A. Hayes – Newington DSO, OBE thanks to the generosity of his daughter Mrs Pat Sheridan and the memories and recollections of former old Rajputs, Majors Hugh Pollen, Frank Wildish, John Mills, Paddy

Lowry, and last but by no means least, Lieutenant Colonel Mustasad Ahmad's book *Heritage* which helped to cor-roborate certain facts. I also was able to refer a number of Regimental Magazines for the year 1945–6. For all this help my grateful thanks.

This story is meant as a tribute to those of the paltan[1] who gave their life for a universally shared idea: peace.

None of this could have been done without the encouragement and typing so willingly undertaken by my late wife, Shirley; my son, Charles, for his editing and help with the manuscript, my daughter, Meryl, for proof reading and my son-in-law, Christopher, for his help with the sketch maps. Any errors or omissions remain mine alone.

Salisbury   Stuart Ottowell
June 2007

---

[1] Group of Soldiers, Viceroy NCOs and Viceroy Commissioned Officers (VCO).

CHAPTER 1

1940–1942:
Frontier Baptism

In the afternoon of 24 February 1992 a car containing three passengers and a driver left the hospitable home and surroundings of Priyanka Farm on the outskirts of Gurgaon in Haryana, the lovely abode of Lieutenant General and Mrs M.L. Thapan. General Thapan had served in 1st and 2nd Rajputs during World War II – but later transferred to the Jat Regiment whose Colonel he subsequently became. We were speeding south, destination Alwar on the borders of Rajasthan, to our host, the 6th (Meiktila) Battalion of the Rajput Regiment. A guide on a motorcycle in the person of Lieutenant Rajesh Kumar Singh, a cheerful personality, was there to see that we stayed on the right road. Beside me sat Lieutenant Colonel Mustasad Ahmad, my friend, volunteer guide and former Commanding Officer (CO), responsible for re-raising the 6th Battalion in 1963. In front with the driver was my son, Major Charles Ottowell, Light Infantry, a serving officer in the British Army.

I had been invited to attend the Meiktila Day and Rangoon Road celebrations, the Battalion's Battle Honours from their previous incarnation when I had had the good fortune and honour to serve with the battalion as a very young officer from August 1942 to December 1945.

We were passing through a fairly flat and featureless countryside and my thoughts went back to the beginnings of this remarkable paltan and my own life with it. I felt that some record of this battalion was very necessary – but how to present it formed the core of my musings as we drove south. Official notes and War Diaries are all very well but they only give overall details of events. The human endeavour is omitted as well as the human failings and it is this, the human factor that was so vital in shaping and making one of the finest battalions in the regiment.

The 6th Battalion of the 7th Rajput Regiment was a wartime-raised unit and because of rapid expansion was woefully short of regular officers though thanks to the fact that the VCOs and NCOs came from other regular units of the regiment, the 'heart' of the battalion was established. Its outlook on work, whatever the task, was best expressed by the phrase 'Dashing Sixth'. All work was done with a will and quickly – we were not ones to linger or grumble about this or that job. The task had to be done so let us do it – *josh*[1] was in good supply!

The Indian Army was an all-volunteer army, and comprised all regular officers, and only some British officers commissioned in wartime, of which I happened to be one. We were there to serve in a battalion of a regiment with the highest traditions of the Indian Army.

In 1940 it was clear that the Indian Army would have to expand to meet the challenges confronting the subcontinent. Lieutenant Colonel Latham, ex Second-in-Command 2nd Battalion/7th Rajput Regiment, was ordered to raise the 6th Battalion in Trichinopoly on 15 July 1940. Drafts of senior VCOs and NCOs from 1st, 2nd and 5th Battalions and the Centre were the nucleus; officers were not plentiful or experienced, however, because most regulars, apart from Colonel Latham were, within the year, to leave for other postings. These were, for instance, Majors Jesty and Gohel, and Captains Pollen and Ranbir Singh.

In spite of this the battalion did well because by the end of 1941 they found themselves in Fort Sandeman where training conditions were more realistic. Major Jesty

---

[1] 'Get up and Go'.

had left and in his place came Major E.C.S. Ward, Captains H. Payne, Wildish, and Lieutenant Nihal Singh. It was whilst the battalion was stationed at Fort Sandeman that we were honoured by a visit from General Sir Claude Auchinleck and subsequently His Excellency the Viceroy who spoke highly of all he saw. Just before moving from Fort Sandeman to Shelabagh, Lieutenant Colonel E.A. Hayes-Newington OBE took over command from Lieutenant Colonel Latham, who was promoted to Brigadier.

The new Colonel had bought two civilian trucks in

Plate 1: Fort Sandeman 1941 – inspection by General Sir Claude Auchinleck.

L. to R. Major Gohel, Captain H. Payne, Captain Rust, Lieutenant Nihal Singh – General talking to Captain Rust. Near figures on right, with back to camera Brigadier Eustace, CO 'Zhob' Brigade – the 'hat' behind is Major E.C.S. Ward, Second-in-Command.

Pishin. At the time the battalion had no transport except mules and horses supplied by the local Animal Transport (AT) Company of the Indian Army Service Corps (IASC). To help in driver training, Captain Ranbir Singh made two wooden dummy gearboxes so that 'changing gears'

Plate 2: Visiting 'School' – where battalion jawans were taught to read and write.

Back of Captain Payne on right, to his left Major E.C.S. Ward.

and 'double de-clutching' (an essential if you wished to change gear downwards in those days) could be practised in preparation of receiving the real thing some time in the future!

The reader may well ask of my own qualifications and reasons for joining the Indian Army and choosing the 7th Rajput Regiment in particular. They are pertinent and require some explanation, though with the benefit of hindsight the whole endeavour rested on the merest chance.

My father Trafford Thomas Ottowell had served throughout the 1914–18 war with the British Army and having been born in Belper, Derbyshire, lived and went to school in Nottingham. On the outbreak of World War I he naturally joined his County Regiment, the Sherwood Foresters or, as it was known, the Notts and Derby Regiment. My much older brother Trafford Roy Mackay (known as Roy), 8 years my senior, went to Sandhurst and was commissioned into the Wiltshire Regiment in the 1930s. By one of those strange coincidences in life, one of his fellow cadets was Nigel Kealey who was commissioned into the Indian Army and eventually joined the 2nd Battalion 7th Rajputs before the war. Long after the war when both my brother and Nigel had retired, they both served as retired officers at Rheindahlen Headquarters in Germany. Having been for some years a member of the 7th Rajput Regimental Dinner Club in London, I knew Nigel Kealey but did not know of any connection between my brother and Nigel until at one of our annual dinners, Nigel asked me if I was any relation to a Colonel Roy Ottowell!

In 1941, when I discovered that my studies in Aeronautical Engineering could be interrupted by compulsory call up, I immediately volunteered for the Army and soon found myself on a Norfolk airfield guarding its perimeter, living in a bell tent and being thoroughly frozen by the chill wind that blew in from the North Sea, straight through the tent and myself.

At eighteen years of age I could not conceive that my chilled presence on a Norfolk airfield in October/November was of the slightest use to the war effort. Fortunately, I was not alone in thinking this way. One of my companions, Anthony R. Gurney,[2] who had also put in his papers for a commission, had a better grasp of what was possible. After a brief telephone call to his home he came back with the astounding news that we should both go and see the Under-Secretary of State for India at the India Office in Whitehall for the purpose of getting a commission in the Indian Army. We assumed the Indian climate would be better than the chill North Sea wind we were experiencing. Our Company Commander very kindly agreed to a 48-hour pass for both of us, and there began my journey.

I embarked, as an Officer Cadet, on the S.S. *Strathnaver* in Glasgow on 4 January 1942. When rounding the Cape

[2] Who joined the 13th Frontier Force Rifles.

of Good Hope I suffered violent pains, which were diagnosed as appendicitis. The troopship had no hospital facilities and therefore I had to wait until we landed at
Durban where I was operated on and, of course missed
the sailing of the ship I had come out on. After con-
valescence I was told to report to Cape Town and board a
cargo vessel bound for Karachi.

On the last leg from Cape Town to Karachi I suddenly
became aware of my complete and utter ignorance of India
as a whole and the Indian Army and its regiments in particular. Fortunately, on the cargo ship I had joined at Cape
Town, were two ex-officers of the Indian Army from the
Great War, one from the 19th Lancers and the other from
the 7th Rajputs. The latter had served with them in the
Middle East and Mesopotamia. On saying goodbye to me
on the dockside in Karachi the ex-Rajput said quietly and
without bombast that the Rajput Regiment was the finest
infantry regiment he had known – so when asked to
give my choice of regiment some three months later in
Belgaum I made the Rajput Regiment my first preference.
I also asked to join an active service battalion. The
authorities were kind enough to grant my requests.

I was commissioned in July 1942 into the Indian Army.
My instructions were to report to the 6th Battalion of the
7th Rajput Regiment. Before I could put this into action I
contracted malignant malaria and retired to the hospital
in the grounds of the Officer Training School (OTS)
Belgaum, where they nursed me through fairly high temperatures until I returned to normal health.

When I left hospital about sixteen days after I had been
commissioned and in a reasonable state of health, I
travelled by train to Poona and then north-west onto
Hyderabad (Sind). The train had left the station and
was heading north to Rohri when the it gradually slowed
down and came to a halt seemingly in the middle of
nowhere! From the top of a railway embankment I saw
that most of the surrounding countryside to our west was

flooded. Fourteen days earlier the river Indus had broken its banks at Sukkar and flooded a stretch of countryside about 10 miles wide at the point of the actual line. The bridge had been badly damaged and the line on either side completely washed away. The railway company had set in motion a very efficient service to carry its passengers across the swollen river. We stopped in the middle of the desert to de-train and get into a fleet of tongas.[3] These took all the railway passengers and their luggage through the shallow water to a fleet of large country boats. Rowers then took us a few miles through deeper water to the river ferries that crossed the main Indus channel. Our progress was quite a cavalcade stretching for over half a mile! The huge expanse of water left the actual river channel indiscernible except for the sight of anchored ferries. These up anchored as soon as we were aboard and conveyed us across the channel to hand us once more to country boats and in turn to more tongas, to splash again through the floods until we met a railway bund to the south of Shikarpur.[4] There, standing patiently was an engine and carriages, which we boarded thankfully and thus found ourselves once more on the main line to Quetta. It was a very impressive response to the disaster that the railway company had just experienced. And an early insight into Indian emergency measures which, whilst slow, worked like clockwork!

Back on the train once more, we found ourselves going through the historic Bolan Pass before reaching Quetta. The broad gauge line continued to Shelabagh, my destination, finally arriving at the portals of the Khojak Tunnel marking the eastern end of the Khojak Pass in Baluchistan, on a sunny afternoon in August 1942. Shelabagh was to be my home until December of that year.

As our train came to a halt at Shelabagh station a

[3] Pony drawn open carriage.
[4] See sketch map of incident.

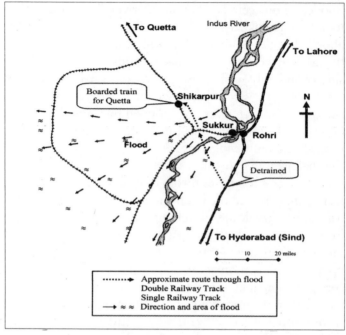

Map 1: Sketch map of the swollen river Indus around
Shikarpur in 1942.

signboard informed passengers that they were at 6,394 ft
above sea level. In front was the gaping mouth of the
Khojak tunnel built in 1888–90, 12,870 ft long – one of
the longest on the subcontinent.

For a young subaltern newly commissioned into the
Indian Army and the Rajput Regiment, in particular, 'Life'
was about to begin. The regiment had been my first choice,
just on the say so of an ex-Rajput officer and fellow
passenger, volunteering his advice on board ship from Cape
Town!

My father and brother were both in British service so I
was not following any family tradition. During my four
months at the Officer Corps Training Unit (OCTU) in
Belgaum I had not heard a single derogatory remark about
the regiment. Thus I knew very little about the regiment

and next to nothing of the 6th Battalion that I was on my way to join. What was the CO like? What were the officers like? What work was the battalion engaged in and would a youngster like me be readily accepted? With a certain amount of apprehension I descended the carriage steps with all my worldly goods: a bedding roll, kitbag and tin trunk.

An officer and orderly appeared from seemingly nowhere and the officer introduced himself as Captain Harry Payne, the Adjutant. He not only showed me to my quarters but also informed me that the battalion was moving out next morning to the Tabina Plateau for a Brigade exercise lasting fourteen days. I would be collected by the transport, a three-ton lorry, in a few days time. Dinner would be at 7 p.m. and the Colonel would see me in the Mess that evening. I would be a Company Officer in B Company which was commanded by 2nd Lieutenant John Mills who had already gone with the advance party to the Plateau. (Lieutenant Mills had joined the battalion at Fort Sandeman.) I was introduced to my orderly, Sepoy Babu Khan, and would share both him and the bungalow with my Company Commander. Having thus briefed me, Captain Payne left me to my own devices, to have a bath, change and go to the Mess before 7 p.m.

On my arrival at the Mess two very jovial Yorkshire men introduced themselves as Ken Crossley and Jack Bateson. I was shown the visitor's book and told to enter my name. As I opened it the very first name in the book was that of a Major Doggrel of the Wiltshire Regiment – he had been my brother's Company Commander in Palestine in 1936 and thus knew much about him. The world was already becoming a smaller place! More officers came in; among whom were Nihal Singh, Chris Perks, Rex Marriott and Bob Child. Next the Colonel, Lieutenant Colonel E.A. Hayes-Newington OBE, came in and I was introduced to him, a tall gentleman, over 6 ft, spare of frame with 'leathery' features, well tanned and in his forties. He was a commanding figure in every sense of the word and for a moment I felt like a fish out of water – somewhat ill at ease and shy. He asked after my ability to speak Urdu and I confessed almost total ignorance. He said that after the brigade exercise I must get down with a Munshi[5] and learn and pass the Urdu exam because none of the Viceroy Commissioned Officers (VCO) would be able to speak to me and I would be unable to converse with them or issue any meaningful orders. And that was that. Not a very promising start, but then at nineteen I did not grieve too much as with the confidence of youth I was sure that things would look better on the morrow.

Sure enough, by the time I had eaten breakfast the following morning the Colonel and the battalion had left except for the Quartermaster Chris Perks, his staff, a Rear party for Quarter Guard duties and the Band. For some reason our Second-in-Command, Major Cecil Ward, was still there and he very kindly invited me to have tea with his wife and two charming daughters aged about 5 and 7. In the shale and poor soil conditions of the station he showed me with great pride a line of tomato plants that were doing very well. No doubt the camel trains that came over the Khojak pass from Kandahar and Chaman provided just the right amount of fertiliser for these plants to survive and thrive! These camel trains came over the pass laden with the most delicious seedless grapes from the vines in and around Kandahar and Chaman and often the bearers would be sent to purchase a few bunches whilst the camels took a breather before descending towards Quetta.

Next day, a tall Havildar[6] came up to me and introduced himself as Shah Mohammed, the transport Havildar. Would I please be ready in 30 minutes as he was taking me to join the battalion. At last I would meet with activity and might become useful. Shah Mohammed was a very

[5] Bilingual Indian teacher of language.
[6] Havildar Sergeant.

skilled driver; the terrain en route was rocky and steep and most bends were beyond the capabilities of our Chevrolet 3 tonner so at least two attempts were necessary to negotiate the many hairpin bends. After some two hours we breasted a pass and came upon a plateau at about 8,000–9,000 ft altitude where the whole battalion was encamped and on a Brigade Exercise – it certainly was a very interesting spectacle.

The battalion had many mules at that time, probably somewhere in the region of forty. They carried our 3-inch mortars, heavy machine guns, signals equipment and, of course, our water and big panniers laden with food, as well as the Mess baggage. The mules were supplied with handlers from the Indian Army Service Corps (IASC) Animal Transport Section from the local area. Everybody seemed to know what they were doing except myself.

I was dropped off in front of a tent and someone said that was where the B Company Commander was. From within, a 2nd Lieutenant John Mills, some three years my senior, was heard letting the world know in a mixture of English and Urdu that he could not find his clothes. Eventually he emerged and introduced himself. An athletic man with broad shoulders, who played cricket, football, and hockey for the battalion, he was obviously very fit and actually spoke less Urdu than I. He was the son of a Rajput officer of the 1st Battalion who had died in the 1920s.

At last I had arrived at a place where there was a job to do! I was quickly disabused of this idea because being a company officer was being 'without' a specific job and at everyone's beck and call.

The Second-in-Command of B Company was a wonderful Viceroy's Commissioned Officer by the name of Subedar Ghulam Ghaus. He was a regular – I forget which battalion he came from originally – but he certainly knew all there was to know about running a company. Our campsite on the Ṭabina Plateau was fairly warm during the day, the sun shone and the sky was cloudless. But in

Plate 3: Shelabagh 1942.

L. – R.: Subedar Ghulam Ghaus Company Second-in-Command,
2nd Lieutenant J.E.G. Mills Company Commander, 2nd Lieutenant
S.D.M. Ottowell Company Officer, Jemadar Rang Khan.

Plate 4: Quetta 1943.

Battalion on parade prior to marching to the station to travel to
Peshawar (before the order 'Fall in the Officers').

the early morning, if you didn't get up quickly enough after the boiling hot water had been poured into your dish for shaving was solid ice in a matter of a quarter of an hour, such was the climate.

The brigade was engaged in an exercise of Frontier Warfare. Speed, precision and timing were all important for success and I had the privilege of seeing an Indian mountain battery gallop into action. The battalion marched in columns across the plateau and ahead of us was a sanger[7] on a hill. The hill was probably 400 ft high and the mountain gunners were called forward to neutralize a supposed enemy on top of the hill. A section of the battery was called up. They came at the gallop and the guns came off the backs of their mules and were in place and firing the first ranging shot within seconds of coming to a halt. It was a spectacular performance; the more so as the ranging shot was bang on target and the whole section, four guns, fired immediately thereafter and obliterated the whole of the top of the hillside. It was a truly magnificent and impressive display of their firepower and accuracy. The battalion would need this kind of shooting if we were to survive over the next two and a half years.

During this exercise much heliograph signalling was practised. Prior to our exercise we had received 'the latest' in mobile wireless sets carried on the backs of the mules of the Signal Platoon commanded by Lieutenant Tommy Harding. Whether it was the altitude, hills or nullahs[8] we shall never know but reception was almost impossible anywhere. 'Helio' however, was surprisingly quick and accurate and we had plenty of sun. The invention of call signs for our new wireless sets gave everyone much amusement and I produce this rhyme as well as I can remember it:

[7] Fortified sentry post.
[8] Dry bed of a seasonal river.

We are the Rajputs straight from the west
Some of the finest and some of the best
We dine like royalty wherever we go
For we are the 6/7th Rajputs

Refrain

Down by that Shela Shela Nullah
You can hear those Rajputs singing
Home Sweet Home
Oh I love to sit and listen
And hear Those Rajputs singing
Home Sweet Home
Way in September the Brig had a dream
So he decided to call it a scheme
So up on Tabina the Rajputs they went
They marched and they marched and they lived in a tent
The call signs of Popeye & Fuffu
Drove everyone barmy
So back over the hills we speedily went
For we are the 6/7th Rajputs.

Very soon it seemed that the exercise was over and we returned to Shelabagh. However, much of our post exercise hilarity was nullified by circumstances out of our control. News reached us that the German Army in southern Russia had broken through the Crimea. There now existed the very real threat that if they were successful and were able to establish themselves in that area they might well try, via southern Russia, to break into Afghanistan. In that event there would be little or no opposition to their armour and we were astride one of the only two entries into India where there were railways (broad gauge) and metalled roads available on entry.

Every rifle company was given a stony slope on either side of the Khojak tunnel overlooking its western portal and was told to dig weapon pits and slit trenches. The ground was loose shale and small slabs of stone but everyone set to with a will. It was very hard work. The slopes were so steep that spoil rolled downhill; besides, being on a forward slope our positions were visible for miles. The whole job was very messy and none of the slit trenches would have been habitable because the shale would collapse whenever you moved about in the trench. However, we did our duty as we saw fit. B Company dug 96 slit trenches and weapon pits. We were all thankful that the Germans found more engaging entertainment nearer home and so left us alone to pursue Frontier Warfare training with all its hazards. I shudder to think what would have happened if they had broken out of the southern Crimea and charged across Afghanistan towards India. Our weapons in those days consisted of SMLE[9] rifles, Bren Guns (one per section) and the heavy machine gun section of the battalion together with 3-inch mortars and 2-inch mortars, which were distributed on the basis of one per platoon!

I had at that time few responsibilities apart from attending B Company office and its parades every morning, going out on route marches, and practising the rudiments of Frontier Warfare with the company.

Another interesting diversion was that all officers used to go to Chaman once a week on two trucks to listen to lectures given by officers of the Gurkhas and our Brigadier on all sorts of subjects. Usually it was topical news, i.e. war news on other fronts. These 'British Officer Hours'[10] as they were called, were really tedious. We learned very little and I think rather resented the fact that the Gurkhas were telling us what was happening. We had our own wireless set in the Mess and knew the world's news as soon as they did. It did not make for good feelings within the brigade. That is, of course, with the benefit of hindsight.

---

[9] Short-Magazine Lee-Enfield.
[10] This term applied to all Commissioned Officers regardless of origin.

What was very amusing was that there were only two officers permitted to drive the two vehicles that took the officers from Shelabagh to Chaman and back. Anyone who knows the route knows that there are some very dangerous hairpin bends on the road and, of course, the road was not macadamized. It was a shale road and liable to slippage on the corners. The two drivers in question were the Colonel and the Military Transport Officer (MTO), Bob Child. The idea was to race each other to Chaman, which meant that the Colonel invariably won the first lap, which is to say out of Shelabagh and onto the mountain road. Once off the mountain road on the other side it was a case of who drove fastest, Child or the Colonel. I must confess that both were experienced fast drivers. But that was really the only excitement of these so-called 'British Officers Hours'! The return journey was no better. Frankly, passengers without exception were glad to get back to the Mess in one piece and have a good stiff drink.

About this time we were joined by a most strange Lieutenant claiming to be an expert in explosives and creating general mayhem behind enemy lines. The Colonel felt that this officer should put on a small course of lectures and demonstrations, first for all VCOs and officers and later for NCOs to attend. The officer in question had just arrived from the UK and to those of us who had not been to the UK since before the war (and this included the Colonel) this Lieutenant simply had to know the latest! Those who had only recently joined and had some experience of wartime conditions and training in the UK were highly sceptical of this officer's claims and accounts; but then we were only subalterns, and so kept our counsel and attended as ordered.

The first lecture and demonstration by this so-called expert confirmed not only my suspicions but certainly brought it home to our Colonel that we would be much safer fighting the Germans than being in the vicinity of this young braggart. His handling of sensitive fuses mixed with gun cotton, his complete lack of understanding of the workings of a Mills hand-grenade, the arming and disarming thereof, and the proximity of fuses to landmines only heightened our concerns about his abilities. It was only, I concluded, under the supreme care of the Almighty that a full complement of VCOs and officers emerged from the hut unhurt and one Lieutenant found himself the following morning entrained for Fatehgarh. The NCOs were thus saved 'instructions' in self-destruction! During wartime it took anything from eighteen months to two years before one was promoted from 2nd Lieutenant to Lieutenant and I think that it was on this account that the Colonel gave this visiting officer his opportunity, never dreaming that he was so extraordinarily inept.

It was now also a time for those officers who wished to pursue careers away from the 6th Battalion to put in their papers for transfer and many left. The Colonel himself was obviously not happy with the performances of some officers and they left as well.

October 1942 came and went and on 11 November, the Bugle Major and his buglers blew the Last Post and the hills around us echoed the wonderful chords. I shall never forget that moment – it was most poignant.

Shortly thereafter I found myself covered in sores and the doctor diagnosed not only what he called Sind sores but also jaundice. I was extremely run down as I'd had a year of considerable illness and I wasn't robust enough to withstand the rigours of change, so I was shipped off to Quetta Hospital. There, thanks to the very good care of the nurses, I recovered sufficiently but not completely by the time December came along.

About a week after the month started an officer in the bed opposite me (a Gunner who also suffered from jaundice) and I were both very fed up with the small progress we were making so we decided to go to the Quetta

Club and cure ourselves with whisky. Which, surprisingly
enough, we did and within a week we were discharged
reasonably fit.

Meanwhile the battalion had left Shelabagh and had
come down to Quetta (5,000 ft) into East Camp. The
weather was bitterly cold and there was snow about. I must
stress that even though the weather was cold at night,
during the daytime very often the sun would heat things
up, unless there happened to be a snowstorm. Quetta as
many will know was the home of the Indian Army Staff
College as well. Senior instructors used to frequently
appear in the club in peacetime Mess kit for which, of
course, we as wartime commissioned officers had no need.
One evening some junior officers of the 6th Battalion were
busy supporting the bar in the club when in strode an
obviously senior Major with bright red pantaloons and a
dark blue patrol jacket which was the Mess dress of the
Baluch Regiment. At that time we didn't recognize him at
all or anything about him – we just thought he was rather
fun with the bright red breeches, but more about him later.
Meanwhile our training consisted of rifle firing on the
ranges, intensive 3-inch mortar firing and much practice
on our Vickers Machine Guns.

Our Colonel was then called away for a month to
Hyderabad (Sind) to assist in the trial of one Pir Pagali, an
alleged troublemaker. A Lieutenant Colonel MacNamara
came to us as caretaker CO and thanks to his sagacity and
experience we saw very little of him. All this arose because
General Headquarters (GHQ) refused the obvious promotion of Captain Harry Payne to Major and Second-
in-Command, and GHQ in their wisdom felt that
without a CO or Second-in-Command we were in need
of succour!

Christmas came and went amongst a lot of festivities
and soon after it was time for us to move on again.

CHAPTER 2

1943–1944: Transport, Mules and Operations on the North-West Frontier

In February 1943 the CO returned and we finally entrained to our new posting – Edwards Lines, Peshawar, North-West Frontier Post (NWFP). Before leaving Quetta by train the General Officer Commanding (GOC) General Monier-Williams came round to each carriage and wished us all well and gave the battalion a 'good chit'.[1]

Arriving in Peshawar it was instant spring. The snow line on the distant Chitral mountains, to the north of us, was going higher every day. Intensive platoon, company training and route marches kept us all on our toes. Our roles in Peshawar were internal security/training and frontier warfare.

We still had no wheeled transport at the time of our arrival, so a civilian contractor was supposed to provide us with seventeen lorries and two cars. Suddenly, one morning I was called into the CO's office and told to take charge of our transport! I was so pleased to get a proper job at last that I quite forgot to inform the Colonel that I knew nothing about it – but upon reflection he must have known.

You can imagine my feelings when I went to the MTO's office to find Havildar Shah Mohammed and L/Naik Maneshwar Prasad Singh present, conferring worriedly and with an air of apprehension. It was a Friday and sitting

[1] Chit – a short official note by the inspecting officers confirming a unit's standards.

on a bench outside was the civilian contractor of our vehicles with a list for me to sign if all was correct, so he could collect the monies owing to him for that week from the paymaster.

Anxious to get the matter over with I turned to Shah Mohammed and asked him if this was correct and that there were seventeen three-tonners and two cars in our lines capable of being used. For an answer he produced his own record of available vehicles that were thus capable: there were two three-tonners and one car! I explained this to the contractor who instantly accused us of plotting against him. When he had calmed down, I invited him to come with me and Shah Mohammed to our MT lines, with the promise that if there were more vehicles that were capable of being used instantly I would of course sign for more. Alas for him, our records were correct and the contractor, after much protest duly departed – but not before I had made it crystal clear to him what our requirements were.

I fear that my predecessor had not troubled himself over the veracity of the records or the petrol account so I had some sympathy with the contractor who was now suddenly obliged to honour his part of the contract with the army because of my arrival as the new MTO. The MT Section was part of HQ Company and as such Captain Rex Marriott was now my Company Commander.

Havildar Shah Mohammed was a very conscientious and serious NCO and his biggest asset to the battalion and myself was that he was able to distinguish between right and wrong and truth and lies and it is fair to say that with few exceptions our senior NCOs throughout the battalion were similarly endowed. Whilst on the subject of personalities, the more youthful L/Naik Maneshwar Prasad Singh, the transport clerk, was outgoing and a pleasant personality but he had to be firmly controlled. His ability to speak English was invaluable in company with Havildar Shah Mohammed, in order to beg, borrow or otherwise acquire the much needed spares to enable us to make 'runners' of the third line vehicles for which the army had no further use. These were finally made available to us at Imphal in 1945. When spares were in short supply at critical times, Maneshwar Prasad had the gifts needed to solve this problem and in these endeavours he always had my full backing. At these times the needs of the battalion and the regiment, had to assume priority above all else. But I race ahead. Suffice to say that eventually all was well and I then went out daily with Shah Mohammed learning to drive, such was my ignorance.

To the east of Peshawar the battalion set up a live firing assault course giving our 3-inch mortars and Medium Machine Guns (MMG) much practice. The system was quite simple in that the sections of the machine-gunners were placed down one side of the course and the 3-inch mortars on a slight rise behind the beginning of the course. They would fire over the heads of the advancing platoons, who were in 'extended order' and would go to ground every 150 yards. The MMGs sited at 200 yard intervals would fire on fixed lines giving the advancing infantry a margin of 5 degrees before they stopped, allowing the infantry to pass and recommence firing, allowing another margin of 5 degrees. A VCO or officer was with every section, though only in a supervisory capacity, to make sure there were no mistakes. There were none and everyone performed faultlessly. This said much for all the training and impressed on all the importance thereof.

As I became fluent in Urdu, the company decided to invite me to eat with them: I was 'on show' sitting at a small table on the veranda of one of our barracks in front of everyone. An awesome experience, but with hindsight a show essential for both sides. The jawans,[2] very shrewd judges, were able to see for themselves what manner of person one of their subalterns was. I was able to see the whole company, recognize some faces I already knew and

[2] Rank of private soldier in the Indian Army.

some that were perhaps new and thus get a broader feel of
the company in which I was serving. After all everyone
was a volunteer, like myself, and for the immediate future
we had a job to do – the business of becoming so good
that no one could ignore our efforts to join actively in
the war raging around us, especially in Burma. Evidently
my performance in Urdu was acceptable *and* I passed my
Urdu test.

To my surprise the Subedar Major (SM), Rahmat Khan,
spoke to me, off duty, and I was able to converse with him
reasonably well to our mutual satisfaction. He had come
from the 5th Battalion and of course was a regular with
many years service and wise in the ways of men. On parade
he was a man of few words but of commanding mien – he
did have a sense of humour and was considered a fair but
strict officer, in fact, everything a SM should be. Sadly he
was no longer young enough to accompany the battalion
on pre-Burma training or subsequently to Burma
itself, and he was missed. His input in India and at the
NWFP had had the desired effect of making the battalion
a cohesive unit, mentally prepared for action. He knew
the CO well and was able to carry out his wishes to the
full.

But I digress. Peshawar was very much a watershed. The
training was basic with an emphasis on personal fitness –
early morning runs for all, route marches and revising
frontier warfare exercises. It should be explained that our
presence in Shelabagh and, for that matter, earlier at Fort
Sandeman was an introduction to the frontier. In that part
of Baluchistan the likelihood of troubles was external rather
than internal and defensive, rather than policing. The
threat of a German advance through southern Russia and
Afghanistan, at that time of the war (1942/3), was a real
possibility. Quetta and Peshawar were, so to speak, 'transit'
areas for us to prepare for the exactitude and 'drill' needed
to be successful in mountain warfare. Also the discipline
thus acquired helped when we found ourselves dealing with
the Japanese later.

Meanwhile in Peshawar we received our first mules – hitherto a mule company from the IASC had supplied our needs both in Shelabagh, Quetta and in the beginning at Peshawar. Each of the Company Commanders were ordered to supply a quota of men for training as mule drivers. Our establishment was for 41 mules and 3 chargers.

Plate 5: One of our mules with the MMG platoon.

In common with most good Company Commanders and their subedars the Animal Transport Section received riflemen from the companies who, in the Company Commander's opinion and that of their Subedars, either did not fit in with the company, were troublemakers, or just odd and perhaps a little too independent. Whatever the reasons, the new recruits to mules that made up our Animal Transport Section had their hands full with half trained animals. The responsibility for grooming, training and cleaning standings[3] all fell on the broad shoulders of Havildar Sheonaik Singh, a senior NCO of much strength but also with a caring attitude to animals and men alike.

---

[3] A place where the mules were shackled, and fed when not in use.

Two years later, when at Imphal our mules were taken from us, the rifle companies to their great surprise received back men who were not only fully trained but capable and able to deal with the business of war. Some fifteen former members of the Animal Transport Section received commendations for bravery and ten were sadly killed in action.

The mules' arrival from the Remount Depot was an occasion when the jawans, sent by the Company Commanders to make up the Animal Transport Section, were watched by the whole battalion. The reception was pure 'spectator sport' and all ranks except our valiant muleteers enjoyed the high spirits of the new arrivals. They pranced, kicked, broke away and generally charged about. Someone had the bright idea of tying empty ghee tins to their tails so that they would trail over their back legs, and lessen the force of the kick, so that the noise might calm our four-legged friends. Finally they ran out of steam and they were led to their standings to be fed and watered and of course shackled (right foreleg to left back leg). I was thankful at the time that the mules and chargers were the sole responsibility of the Quartermaster, one Captain Portugal.

Officially, since leaving Shelabagh we had not had a Battalion Second-in-Command after Major Ward's promotion to command another Rajput Battalion. Major Harry Payne, our only other Senior Regular Officer apart from the CO, had been officiating since; he was well liked by all ranks – but it was not to be and a Major R.M. Hall (also a regular) was posted in and took up his appointment with us in Peshawar. At a makeshift Durbar[4] he was introduced to everyone.

One incident I recall from our days in Peshawar was indicative of our concern for others. In early summer Peshawar can become very hot and on one of these days rumour had it that the 2nd Battalion was passing through

[4] All ranks formal meeting.

by train on their way to Landi Kotal from Burma. So, upon confirmation, large quantities of tea were made and transported to the station and distributed with some food amongst the ranks of the 2nd Battalion. One of its Company Commanders was a young Captain by the name of M.L. Thapan – who later became a close friend of the writer.

In August/September the battalion received orders to move to Damdil on the famous Bannu-Razmak Road. This was our first real taste of the Frontier and everyone was excited and thrilled to be moving 'up the ladder' in being recognised by the powers at GHQ that the 6th were capable of playing their part. We were, frankly, fed up with all the training and Peshawar in particular. In moving us to Damdil GHQ were beginning to recognize the importance of our battalion and it made everyone feel that our hours of training, courses and runs were not going to waste and that when tested we would not be found wanting. Our move from Peshawar was not, however, without incident.

To reach the railway station at Peshawar we had to use our civilian three-tonners for all baggage and the last vehicle was inevitably overloaded – Sepoy Hari Singh was its driver and I, the passenger. All went well until we started going down hill towards the bazaar when suddenly there were no brakes. The handbrake did not work and Hari Singh initially tried to engage a low gear to slow down our speed. As he did so the top of the gearbox and gear-handle came away as all the bolts had rattled loose! Hari Singh managed to engage a lower gear with the end of the gear lever, and to get the lid and gear lever back. I crouched down on top of the gearbox (now loose) and held the gear lever in position while Hari Singh managed the vehicle round the bend at the bottom of the hill. From then on it was flat to the station. We were both relieved that the journey was over! I leave you to guess what I said to the contractor responsible for maintenance.

The battalion was glad to be moving towards a more active role and putting all its frontier warfare training to some real use. We travelled by train via Lahore to Mari Indus and from there we transferred to a narrow gauge railway known throughout the frontier as 'The Heatstroke Express'. The distance was about 80 miles and the actual travelling time was about six hours. Two complete trains moved the battalion. About halfway there was a junction called Lakhi Marwat where everyone could get out, have a meal and cool drink and re-enter those very hot carriages to continue to Bannu, arriving about 4 p.m. At that time anywhere was better than those small railway carriages which were filled to bursting with humans, kit and mules. The train was aptly named!

At Bannu we were informed that the road would be 'open' in two days time which gave everyone a chance to recall the purpose of our journey, to get to Damdil and drop one company off at a lonely fort called Thal, over-looking the valley of the Tochi River at the bend of the road which then ran up into the hills towards Damdil about 12 miles away. The whole battalion was in a large convoy of trucks owned by a civilian contracting firm called the Baggai Lorry Service who did the run from Bannu via Miran Shah, Damdil, Gardai and Razmak and return on Road Open Days only. In some places the bends and gradients were very reminiscent of the 'road' between Shelabagh and Chaman. Some were single track with few passing places. The lorries were very well maintained and the Pathan drivers superb. Passenger comfort was nil but one could hang on to the superstructure.

One place of note we passed by was the RAF station at Miran Shah, which was the station at which A/C Shaw (Colonel T.E. Lawrence of Arabia) served in the 1920s.

We were escorted all the way by a squadron of armoured cars from 16th Light Cavalry (World War I Rolls Royce armour plated cars with a MMG mounted cupola on top).

Plate 6: Officers and VCOs of the 6/7th Rajputs in Peshawar, 1943.

Back Row:
Lieutenants Munchi, Levine and Williams, 2nd Lieutenant
Ottowell, Lieutenants Battacharya and Harding.
Second Row:
Lieutenant Child, Jemadar Abdul Haq, Captain Crossley,
Subedars Kedar Singh and Mohammed Afsar, Jemadar Wahib
Din, Captain Bateson, Jemadars Maldeo Singh and Rang Khan,
Captain Nihal Singh and Lieutenant Jain.
Sitting:
Captain Portugal, Subedar Ghulam Ghaus, Captain Payne,
Subedar Major Rahmat Khan OBI, Lieutenant Colonel
Hayes-Newington OBE Commanding Officer, Subedar
Pralad Singh, Captains Cox and Marriott.
Absent on Courses:
Lieutenants J. Knox and J. Boon, Captain Perks and
Lieutenant J.E.G. Mills.

We stopped at Thal Fort and Major Jack Cox and D
Company was selected to do the first month's stint on
their own.

We arrived in Damdil, a stone walled encampment
containing a small hospital, the 14/14th Punjabs and a

Plate 7: Damdil Camp, Spring 1944.

Far left, the 14/14th Punjab Regiment campsite; near centre the Medical Centre consisting of 4 huts; far centre the campsite of the 6/7th Rajputs with their transport lines and four wheeled carriers; near right is the guard on top of the Rajput Fort with a 3-inch mortar, to his right the Bannu–Razmak Road – Bannu being through the gap in the hills in the distance.

section from 16th Light Cavalry Armoured Cars commanded by Captain Jimmy Bowen and Lieutenant Abdul
Gaffur Khan.

We were part of the Gardai Brigade,[5] which consisted
of 4 battalions plus artillery 25 pounders in support and
the 16th Light Cavalry, all commanded by Brigadier
Hobbs. He had met us at Chaman the previous year when
he was commanding the Gurkhas and we were warmly
welcomed.

Our Battalion Transport Section now consisted of four
3-ton Chevrolets plus two 15-cwt Fords and four 4-wheel
open top carriers with 5 ft diameter wheels. The armour
plating on these carriers was so designed that if you happened to be tall, and were seated when the driver applied
his brakes suddenly (which were not only hydraulic but
also vacuum assisted), decapitation could seal your fate in
a second! They were certainly lethal for the occupants.
Whether these vehicles were lethal to their enemies will
always remain a debatable point. We were lucky to avoid
such accidents though there were plenty of bruises. Two
of these carriers were reliable but it took hours of work to
make the other two serviceable. When we succeeded we
hoisted pennants, by command of the MTO, and the
battalion then had a carrier platoon.

At Damdil it was 'suggested' that the QM had a lot to
do and that perhaps I might look after the mules. Whilst
the performance the mules gave in Peshawar was very
amusing for the onlooker the reality was very far from
being funny and since it was only the QM throwing out
hints I objected in no uncertain terms, much to everyone
else's amusement.

I should have known better! Within two months I found
myself on an Animal Transport Course in Jullundar
and 41 mules and 3 chargers became my responsibility

---

[5] This was a 4 battalion brigade as opposed to the usual
3 battalion brigade.

thereafter as well. If it had not been for the understanding, knowledge, and sheer hard work of Havildar Sheonaik Singh, correct feed, daily training and of course *malish*,[6] most of our mules would not have been able to carry such a diversity of equipment such as MMGs, 3-inch mortars, signalling equipment, water, rations and in fact anything that could be tied or hung from a mule's packsaddle.

The mules and the chargers were only as good as their feet and these were shod by a person who appeared to me as a newcomer to be an 'old soldier' – that is until you saw his hands and his extraordinary ability to shoe the wildest mule with an air of calmness and authority which every animal understood. His cold shoeing and fitting was a pleasure to watch and throughout the time he was working on an animal he would be talking to it non-stop in a language which bore only the slightest resemblance to Punjabi. His swearing, however, was loud and clear and usually directed at the unfortunate sepoy mule-driver holding the mule's reins. Sowar Haider Khan was our farrier and as such was on our strength. The Colonel, more than most of us, at that time realized Haider Khan's skill and he was made up to a Lance Duffadar[7] to give him some monetary recompense for his ability, and such was his standing within the battalion that even the Colonel would only ever 'request' of him to do so and so. He was never ordered to do a job; he was, as with so many members of the 6th, thinking ahead about how to solve the next problem. Equally obvious, with a man of Haider Khan's dedication to his craft, all mule-drivers were told to report any loose shoes directly to the farrier. It was also just as well that Haider Khan enjoyed robust health!

In Damdil also, the natural instincts of one shy and most unprepossessing jawan came to light in the guise of L/Naik Driver Jai Singh. This extraordinary man when

[6] Grooming.
[7] Cavalry or mounted version of the rank for Lance Naik.

asked to intervene in a battle between a driver and his non-starting vehicle would lift the bonnet, place his nose and head under it and quietly and unerringly put matters right and so restore peace. He had had no formal training, attended no courses, but always put his finger on the problem. He was a man of few words, but when an engine burst into life a smile would light up his whole face, which said it all. He was able to report good and bad news almost without emotion and he ably assisted Havildar Shah Mohammed in all matters mechanical.

My mechanical experience had been gained on an extensive course on Internal Combustion (IC) engineering at the Chelsea Engineering College and the relatively simple IC engines we had were no mystery to me. Jai Singh and I spent many hours on heavy maintenance, which really flew in the face of army regulations and we were no doubt contravening every order about what we could and could not do when it came to maintenance. But our nearest depot for repair was either Razmak or Bannu and we could not afford to lose vehicles for weeks on end to change such things as cylinder head gaskets, leaking water-pumps, broken half-shafts, bad timing, etc. Strictly speaking and according to army regulations we could have been charged with contravention and be heavily fined, but the Colonel had to have transport that worked and to my knowledge he never raised any objection. We just indented for spares which should not have been delivered to a battalion, but which came nevertheless! We did not know of our Light Aid Detachment Indian Electrical and Mechanical Engineers (LAD IEME) and with hindsight they did not bother about us. It all meant that we were in charge of our affairs and not dependent on others.

I have to pause here to remind the reader that in spite of the age of our transport there were strict orders about what a unit's MT section was permitted to do and what not to do. I have to admit that the latter was never up-permost in my mind and to my best knowledge we never submitted a vehicle to any IEME workshop unless it had been in an accident and needed a major repair or re-place-ment of say an engine or body.

Unfortunately, this way of carrying on, though never causing the Colonel or myself any twinges of conscience, finally caught up with me when I was called in by the Colonel IEME at 17th Divisional HQ at Nyaunglebin in Burma in September 1945. He confronted me with the startling fact that neither the LAD IEME nor divisional workshops had in eight months ever seen one of our ve-hicles and by whose authority were big ends being re-placed? I said that as MTO I was that authority and he snapped back that I had no qualifications. I murmured that I had done nine months on aero-engines, radial and inline, at Chelsea Aeronautical College before joining the war effort and was qualified to hold down the job of 'Inspector before Flight' – this took him straight on to 'where did I get my spares from'. That of course was a secret safely held and kept by our MT Section! 'Why were we two vehicles over establishment and where had they come from and was I not aware of army regulations covering these subjects and of course because we were two vehicles over establishment I was contravening our petrol allowance and that this matter would be taken higher!' I said 'Yes Sir', saluted smartly and departed at great speed to report this to my Colonel, now Brian Montgomery, who promptly rang Lieutenant Colonel Wilfred Miron the AQ of Division. He was the only Senior Divisional Staff Officer with us throughout the Burma Campaign and a friend of the battalion, who simply told us 'not to worry'. We never heard another bleep, and we kept our two vehicles.

Whilst Jai Singh and I laboured on our vehicles, when the road was not 'open', the 'brains' in the battalion decided to design and build 'The Rajput Fort'.[8] It was an imposing

---

[8] A defended watchtower covering part of the route built by the battalion.

structure and Captain Chris Perks was the main architect with suggestions from all present. It was 'Do It Yourself' on a grand scale and I know that several VCOs and NCOs who claimed knowledge of building volunteered to raise the stone walls. It was of squarish plan and the intention was to be able to mount and to fire one of Subedar Kedar Singh's 3-inch mortars from the roof! When finished the Colonel gave permission for the mortar to be fired. We only realized afterwards that our roof could not take the recoil happily, so a sentry was mounted beside the mortar and with both visible the *dushman*[9] would not know of our secret but see the warning clearly enough.

One day we had an inspection by the GOC NW Army, Lieutenant General Buckley. As always the battalion behaved impeccably and he stayed the night and dined in the Mess with nine officers present. Others were away on courses and leave. Now General Buckley's chief hobby and table talk was about fishing – unhappily the writer's knowledge of fish of any kind, large or small, only extends to what he ate. Because I was the most junior member of the Mess the Colonel asked me to sit on the left of our illustrious guest – he, the Colonel, would sit on the right side. What I did not know at the time was that every officer had been asked to sit in my seat and all had declined! I passed food and made all the polite noises one is supposed to, but in vain – General Buckley would only converse about fishing so there was an inevitable end to our communications. In defence it has to be said that there were not many officers in the Indian Army to reach high rank who could not converse on practically any topic with their hosts because, of course, 'shop' in the Mess, even ours, was taboo.

Whilst at Damdil I was detailed to run a Driving and Maintenance Course for the whole Gardai Brigade at Dera Ismail Khan (DIK). DIK as it was known is on the river

[9] Urdu for 'enemy'.

Indus at the edge of the Sind Desert and at the beginning
of the road going to Tank and Wana in Waziristan. It came
within the boundary of the NW Frontier and was strictly
a liquor forbidden area.

I had a Camp Commandant, a regular officer from the
Lincolnshire Regiment by the name of Major Fox whose
sole contribution was to see that our tented accommodation was 'in order'. I was told to do 'whatever I was
supposed to do'. So I drew up a simple daily programme
of PT first thing, breakfast, theory, maintenance on
vehicles, and training drivers in convoy. It has to be
remembered that most drivers were new to driving but
each unit had supplied experienced drivers for the vehicles
and NCO instructors. One of the units had supplied my
Second-in-Command, a Subedar. I believe he came from
the Dogra Regiment. DIK in winter, and this was
December, could be extremely hot during the day but
cooled rapidly in the late afternoon and evening. The
cookhouse or *langar* had to cater for six or seven differing
castes and religions – there were Hindu Rajputs, Punjabi
Musalmans, Sikhs, Gurkhas, Garhwalis, Jats, and Dogras.

Our daily work ended at 5.30 p.m. By 6 p.m. on one
day the Subedar Sahib came to see me just as I was ready
to dress to go out to the club – the Subedar wore a very
troubled mien, which communicated itself to me without
him saying anything. I was instantly on the alert. He
explained that the Sikh contingent were bent on creating
trouble and had started an argument in the *langar* and to
me that was bad news. For the reason, I have to take the
reader back to my journey as an Officer Cadet from Cape
Town to Karachi.

As we were saying our farewells on arrival at Karachi
one of our fellow travellers, the ex-officer from the Rajputs
who had commended the Rajput Regiment to me, then
said a curious thing. 'If you ever command Sikhs, it is in
their and your interest to keep them occupied 25 hours
out of 24!' I had pondered that saying and thought nothing

very much of it but with the Subedar Sahib sitting opposite me looking extremely worried I suddenly realized the implications.

Our course programme during the day was a busy one and left most of us tired by 5.30 p.m., having started at 7 a.m. It was immediately obvious to me that the Sikh contingent had had too much idle time on their hands in spite of a ten hour day. So I ordered the Sikh contingent to parade in full Field Service Marching Order, which meant packs as well, and I was similarly dressed. They thought this strange at 6 p.m. I believe they thought it was an inspection! I quickly disabused them thereof because having ported arms we right turned and it was 'double march' for the next two miles – marching for two more miles and 'double march' for the last mile. They were short of breath when we arrived back at camp. I then asked them if they had any complaints about their food – the answer was none.

The senior NCO, a Havildar who was in charge of them, asked me if they could be dismissed. I said certainly, providing they gave an unequivocal assurance that they stopped causing any trouble in the *langar* or elsewhere. This they started to discuss. As there was obviously still some doubt in their minds I ordered them to 'Ground Arms and take their equipment off' and we right turned and were off for a five mile run non-stop. It so happened that I was fit and capable of this routine but the Sikhs were obviously much troubled. The last mile or so I ran at the rear, as fall outs were not permitted! We finally arrived back in camp and I posed my question again. This time there was no discussion or hesitation and the Havildar apologized on their behalf and gave me the required assurance. I had no further problems from these very intelligent members of the course.

But I digress. Christmas 1943 in Damdil was celebrated by playing a football match against 14/14th Punjab, who shared the camp with us. Several of our officers, notably

Jack Bateson, Tommy Harding, John Mills, John Knox and Maldeo Singh were, by our standards, good and our movement was always forward towards the 14/14th goal and we succeeded in winning by a small margin. The Colonel of the 14/14th who at that time was the only Lieutenant Colonel on the Station and therefore the Senior Officer, was not amused and our Second-in-Command, Major Hall, received an unfriendly lecture from the Punjab Colonel afterwards. I distinctly remember the Subedar Major however, was pleased at the result and so we all retired to our own part of the camp. The football pitch was outside the perimeter on a flat piece of ground devoid of any vegetation and very hard. It has to be admitted that we were a very boisterous lot when not on parade.

THE CAKE

Sepoy Mohammed Sharif was a tall well-built soldier, smart in appearance and very punctilious in carrying out his duties. In common with most sepoys Mohammed Sharif spoke no English and understood none and there the matter would have rested to the end of our lives had it not been for a cake. His 'misfortune' was that he had agreed to be orderly to two British Rajput Officers on the North West Frontier with the 6th Battalion of the 7th Rajput Regiment stationed at Damdil.

On 25 January 1944, the battalion was out on Road Open duties, guarding the hills on either side of the road to Razmak. At that time of the year the days were hot but the nights were cool. When we finally returned to camp, hot, dusty and tired, Mohammed Sharif, who had stayed behind as part of the camp guard, was told to prepare our two baths. Suddenly it occurred to the writer that the morrow would be his 21st birthday and we would be in camp, so the baths waited as Sharif was despatched to fetch the Mess cook at once in order to be given the necessary instructions for a birthday cake.

Plate 8: The Cake!

L. to R.: 2nd Lieutenant S.D.M. Ottowell and the Mess Cook.

Five minutes went by and after about ten minutes Sharif returned with a somewhat careworn expression saying that the cook could not come. My brother officer was appalled that the cook had calmly brushed aside an order given by an officer! Clearly, there was some misunderstanding and Lieutenant Mills most emphatically ordered Mohammed Sharif to 'Bring the cook here'! Sharif departed, albeit reluctantly, and returned very shortly without the cook.

We were both tired very frustrated, and by then undressed to get ready for a cleansing bath. Nevertheless the annoyance of an unfulfilled order meant that Mohammed Sharif received the full fury of a twin verbal dressing down from two subalterns dressed in towels. Like a good Rajput he withstood all this with great composure. When we finally ran dry and our Urdu vocabulary ran out, a certain pause and stillness set in. Into this quiet Mohammed Sharif injected, calmly and in perfect English, his own very explicit thoughts about the cake that had caused him so much trouble. We were so astonished to hear it in English from him and so well understood his feelings, that we just roared with laughter, had our bath, and forgot all about the cake.

Next day to my very great surprise and pleasure the cook produced a very fine three-tier cake made at the ex-press order of the Commanding Officer the day be-fore!! And Sepoy Mohammed Sharif had been sworn to secrecy! We had the grace to apologize to our orderly – we could hardly do less.

In February we moved 'up the road' and joined the Razmak Brigade. Thus we experienced hutted accommo-dation for all and the Station also boasted a small bazaar. We used to 'open the road' up to and including the Razmak Narai[10] and elements of the Gardai Brigade would meet with us there to complete the chain of protection we gave the road.

In 1943/4 the 'Fakir of Ipi' was creating some trouble though he never seemed to show when we were on duty except once and it was on the occasion when our four wheeled carriers were running well. The signal to retire had been given at the end of the afternoon and the outlying pickets were coming in when suddenly to the north of the *narai* some shots were fired in our general direction. The carriers right wheeled, crossed a small nullah and came out onto a reasonably flat terrain to give cover to one of our retiring pickets and to see if we could get near the origin of the firing. Alas when we met the picket, wireless orders had been received from the Colonel to abandon the chase and return. So the picket received a free ride back.

Shortly after this episode we were issued with four new tracked Bren gun carriers. These we had to collect from the railhead at Mari Indus in the full heat of June where temperatures in daytime were 120 degrees plus and at night time only a little below 90 degrees Fahrenheit! As the carriers were all metal we could only deal with them between 5 and 6 a.m. in the morning. Three of them started but the fourth kept us there for another 48 hours! We tried to

[10] Gully.

work at night but the lack of good lighting delayed us and dawn was such a short period before the sun came up and quite mercilessly 'burnt' us off the carrier. The whole petrol feed system had to be cleaned including tank, carburettor and pump.

None of us had ever driven a carrier so there in the desert above the Indus at Mari Indus we learned how to control the two levers which, if correctly applied, would enable one to turn right or left as required. The secret was to apply the correct pressure for the turn and when we got onto tarmac just the slightest touch would have us round 360 degrees in no time. Fortunately we all had a light touch and so we drove from Mari Indus via Bannu and a 'Road Open Day' all the way to Razmak. At the end of that journey we had four very experienced Bren gun carrier drivers. But as so often happened, having acquired these skills we left the carriers behind and never again were required to use them!

Plate 9: On a 'Road Open Day' 1944.

On the left is the road to Damdil and then Razmak, to the right is the road to Bannu via the Thal Fort where D Company was stationed. Centre right, an armoured car and to its right an armoured personnel carrier and 3-tonner. All vehicles were from the 16th Light Cavalry.

August–September saw the battalion on the move again – this time it was jungle training in preparation for the war proper. The place selected for us was Bethmangla in Mysore State, southern India about 6 miles from the Kolar gold fields. The journey by train was uneventful for the battalion but for 41 mules, a complement of 50 men, myself and an orderly it was a 14 day ordeal and especially for our poor animals, thanks to the 'passive civil disobedience campaign' then running in central and southern India. The animals suffered most because they were in all metal trucks, with daytime temperatures inside well over 110 degrees Fahrenheit, in spite of open doors. We were constantly, without our knowledge, being unhooked at night from our train until we set up a rope alarm system that would tell the sentry on duty – who held one end of the rope and was in the last carriage (where we all slept) – when we were being unhooked! As a result the food arrangements for the animals became non-existent. So we bought where we could and whatever was available, at all our stops. Because of the refusal of some officials to even countenance our journey south by main line, we were obliged to make detours – hence there were no food arrangements for the animals.

Station Staff Officers (SSO) at some of the main line stations became curiously 'unavailable'. Havildar Sheonaik Singh was a tower of strength throughout and all jawans gave of their best in the most trying circumstances – full of provocation – but we had our mules to think of and so we 'talked' our way south. Our frustrations were beginning to manifest themselves at Kalyan Junction. Here we expected to break our journey because the train we came in on was destined for Bombay and we had to continue south via Poona. Havildar Sheonaik Singh and myself went to see the Station Master to ask for his co-operation in having our trucks attached to the Night Mail to Poona and to find accommodation on the train for those of us not on duty.

It was here that we at last discovered the real reason for all our misfortunes to date, the 'civil disobedience campaign'. The Station Master informed us that he could hardly be expected to raise a finger to assist us whether this meant food and water for our mules, shunting of our transport, or, indeed, onward transportation for us. And of course we were not allowed to help ourselves without his express permission! I happened to catch a glimpse of an SSO crossing the footbridge to come to our aid; but alas, from afar he could see our problem and immediately did a smart about turn and departed speedily. He obviously knew what problems were facing us and perhaps just felt that the day had been too hot for him to take on more. We thus never saw him again.

Meanwhile we refilled our *chagals*[11] and water containers for the mules from the tap on the platform and while this was going on I saw a lone shunting engine waiting for a signal in the yard. I approached and asked for the driver's help to move the trucks off the main line to a siding in the hopes that the same driver and engine would be available to reconnect us to the rear of the Poona Express after its arrival. To my surprise and relief he promised both things including the persuasion of the signal box to give him the necessary free road! I certainly had not expected this and thanked him and his fireman. These arrangements were completed long before the Poona Express was due. So on it's arrival 'our' shunter was able to bring our mule trucks round and the fireman, whose duty it was not, very kindly helped to hook our trucks safely on the back of the Express.

Suddenly the Station Master appeared and said that he would not allow this unauthorized action of ours and he would have us uncoupled. I immediately posted an armed guard at the coupling and invited the Station Master to find us some 30 seats in the last carriage, which was well filled – one might almost say overcrowded. He laughed, turned on his heel, and headed for his office.

[11] Canvas water bottle.

Meanwhile this whole episode had been witnessed by all the passengers of the last carriage who were ever curious of the drama unfolding in front of their eyes. I felt that the 6/7th had just about stood enough – we were not in politics. We understood that everyone had a duty to perform and that included us, and we had no intention of straining the obligation of hospitality of Kalyan Junction or its Station Master to breaking point so our departure had to take place.

In those days the drill of 'Fix Bayonets' was, if well done spectacular. The precision with which our jawans performed the movement on Kalyan Station was as One – they were certainly not going to let the regiment down by sloppy drill. Our audience in the carriage enjoyed the sight as a piece of theatre, understood our need, had heard the Station Master's rebuttal of our request and as the jawans had come to the 'High Port' with bayonets fixed, voluntarily vacated the whole carriage so that all of us had seating without conflict with the civilian passengers who promptly returned both to the interior of the coach and the roof. Thus calm was restored, as well as good humour – our jawans were always good diplomats!

The Station Master, to his fury, was obliged to let the Poona Express plus our trucks leave on time! Our real concern remained for our 41 mules that had so far been eleven days on the journey, from Lahore at the height of the summer with the wrong or no food. Their condition was deteriorating rapidly and any prospects of a proper diet in these conditions were nil. Fortunately railway stations always possessed passable drinking water for them and plenty of it.

When we finally arrived, the Colonel came to Bethmangla station to greet us, much to everyone's relief. It took us one month to get the animals fit again.

At Bethmangla the paltan got down to jungle training very seriously and everyone had to be fit – morning runs and physical training exercises were the order of the day. War establishments were studied and we could now indent for stores, which hitherto had only been issued after the most careful enquiry. Naik Maneshwar Prasad Singh was in his element and we indented for whatever we thought we would need and what is more we got most of it which was promptly locked away in a steel cabinet against our future need. Our Farrier, Haider Khan, received a travelling anvil and a good supply of shoes and nails. About a week after, we received some new replacement mules from the Remount Depot and then had a tragedy that touched us all. One of the new intake of mules had almost perfect conformation but was a little highly strung. The mule driver and all of us made probably more fuss over it but after a good *malish* the sunlight would reflect from its coat which was a fresh chestnut colour. It always made a good showing on the Commanding Officer's inspection, once a month, on a Wednesday. To start with we had to tether the mule away from the rest, as it had a ferocious kick especially reserved for its fellow mules. One early morning at about 2.30 we had a very severe thunderstorm – much lightning but not much rain. This mule was shackled in the normal way as it was not on the standings, but separated from the rest. It broke its rear shackle and then proceeded to wind itself with its front leg shackle around the tree until it would turn no more. In its frenzy it broke its shoulder – the 'Stick Guard' had seen this and told Havildar Sheonaik Singh, but by then it was too late. The animal had obviously been beside itself during the thunder and lightning and afterwards it was quite still supporting itself on three legs. Every bone had been broken in the shoulder and the leg was back to front. I consulted the Colonel. A grave was dug to take the mule and very gently we coaxed it to stand parallel to its grave and I had to kill the animal with my .45 colt pistol. On my animal training course in Jullundar, the instructor had been most specific in such an eventuality; an imaginary line between the inner corner of the left eye to the right ear and vice versa. Where these lines crossed was was the 'Point' but the muzzle of the revolver had also to be at the right angle with the forehead!

I did as instructed and the mule ended its suffering instantly; it was a bruising experience for us all.

Whilst busily training at Bethmangla, all our Weapon Officers and VCOs were armed with revolvers with which to defend themselves. So higher authorities sent us a Mr Taylor who was an expert in personal weapons. He was reputed to be an excellent shot having been loaned to the New York Police Department in the 1930s to deal with a notorious gangster called Dillinger. The problem was that this villain knew how to protect himself when walking in broad daylight. For instance he always made sure that his 'girlfriend of the day' would be by his side on the roadside – thus offering the smallest target to anyone seeking to kill him – otherwise he was well guarded by his bodyguards fore and aft. To apprehend him normally was not possible. Some policemen had already been killed. Given that the target was so well protected and that the police could not afford to shoot and accidentally kill or wound the girlfriend, other means had to be found. It must be remembered that in the 1920s and 1930s the USA suffered a plague of this kind of gangster in many of their larger cities. Mr Taylor was asked to view this prospect in New York and he found that the task though difficult was within his capability and remember the distance was from a doorway on the other side of the road (avenue) some 50 yards. He succeeded to everyone's relief! He gave us all some useful hints, such was his expertise with the revolver and rifle.

One day we were honoured by the visit of no less a person that the GOC Southern Army, Lieutenant General Berisford-Pierse. Everything went well, he visited all our companies and finally all Officers and VCOs were there to see him off. Suddenly the General, in front of us all, turned to our Colonel and said 'Crazy,[12] how old are you?'

---

[12] An affectionate name applied by all, to the style of command by Lieutenant Colonel Hayes-Newington.

The Colonel gave his correct age, whereupon the General said, 'you are too old to go into battle!' We were stunned. The Colonel, to his eternal credit, said nothing, saluted, and the General departed.

Within 48 hours of that exchange the whole battalion was outside Southern Army Command area en route to Ranchi to join the famous 'Black Cats', the 17th Indian Light Division commanded by Major General 'Punch' Cowan. Thereafter the Colonel was seen in a different light: suddenly we became aware of the old saying 'better the devil you know than the devil you don't'.

Ranchi was for us the final testing ground to see to individual fitness and aptitude of everyone – the section, platoon, company and battalion. We tested our new equipment, sten guns, jeeps, 15 cwt trucks, new wireless sets, saying goodbye to our chargers and concentrating on our 41 mules, loading them into lorries and unloading them. After many practices all could be loaded in less than 8 minutes, tailboards up and engines started and unloaded in under 10 seconds!

We had trained our mules to jump safely from the backs of the lorries led by drivers so there was no need for ramps. It was a most impressive display and I think the mules enjoyed it too. They were also ridden bareback for physical training in the mornings before their breakfast, which was enjoyed by all.

Visiting Generals and senior Veterinary Corps Officers all gave us 'good chits'. But then the same thing could be said of all rifle companies and the whole paltan. Everyone knew their task and if possible the 'other' person's as well.

It was thus, on a high note, that we started our long journey into Burma, via Calcutta, Guahati, Dimapur and Kohima to Imphal. This is where most of our ideas and schemes changed direction with bewildering speed and we had to be flexible enough to cope without appearing to be surprised or seeming incapable of handling the situation.

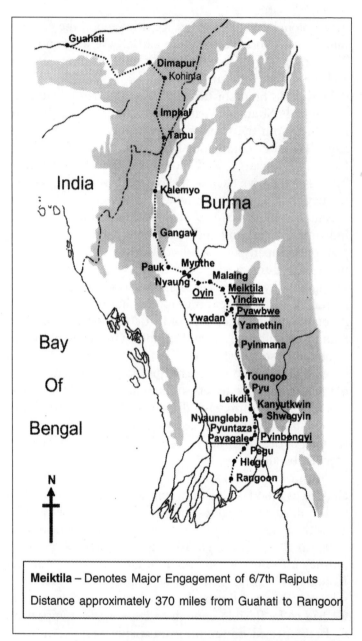

Map 2: Sketch map of Burma in the 1940s.

CHAPTER 3

1945: Meiktila – The Masterstroke

Once we were across the mighty Irrawaddy River, in the context of our subsequent involvement, it is important to understand how 14th Army's planning of the operation called EXTENDED CAPITAL[1] sought to draw our enemy into central Burma, thereby affording our armour maximum flexibility, superiority and manoeuvrability to deal effectively with our enemy. Japanese intelligence's own assessments of our movements and strengths were in most cases minimized and wrong. Their commanders were inclined because of this to ignore the reports. To make matters worse for them a dummy Corps Headquarters was set up to give them a picture that IV Corps was going to cross the Irrawaddy to give our forces towards Mandalay help and reinforcement. Crossing as we did at Pagan enabled us to strike at Meiktila before the Japanese High Command could do anything about this thrust. Their major supply depot and communications centre at Meiktila was exposed and IV Corps and 6/7th Rajputs, in particular, captured it; thus denying the enemy sorely needed rations, ammunition and the facilities of a major field hospital. Then, when Mandalay fell, the Japanese 33rd Army under

[1] General Slim's first objective in planning the recapture of Burma, with the resources available to him, was to capture Mandalay (CAPITAL) and whilst the enemy forces were concentrating on fighting this threat, IV Corps including 17th Indian Division were to cross the Irrawaddy River to the south and attack Meiktila (EXTENDED CAPITAL).

General Honda, sought to recapture Meiktila to shorten
their lines of communication. Thankfully the sharp thrust
of the Kabaw Valley campaign removed the likelihood of
any interference by the remnants of the 15th Japanese
Army, under General Nataguchi in central Burma. That
army became embroiled in the vast jungle and hills of the
Pegu Yomas only to emerge after the monsoon had started
as a disease ridden band of refugees at Nyaunglebin, and
were taken prisoner by the 6/7th Rajputs.

Clearly, apart from assembling his army near suitable
starting places, General Slim had to test out the likelihood
in regard to his plans for success with the actual material
available to him. He was not in any position to order all
he needed; for instance, had we had just one tank with a
flail attached, many of our casualties could have been
avoided, both of men and tanks. Flail tanks were in
abundance in Europe at that time. Our enemy was adept
at digging small holes to take a 250 lbs aerial bomb plus
one man crouching over the striker with a stone ready to
strike and so detonate the bomb should a tank go over
him or troops be very close. They camouflaged these holes
superbly.

The Colonel came back one morning from his briefing
at Divisional HQ to announce that all mules would be
returned and we were immediately to adjust ourselves
to be a parachute battalion to be dropped ahead of our
advance! So load tables were studied all day and night, the
reallocation of men, weapons and material determined,
and of course, the Colonel had to raise important questions
such as when and where and means (parachute packs). We
thus said goodbye to our mules. The following day, instead
of further developments, the Colonel then came back and
told us that we would be used as glider borne troops. So
there were more load tables to study!

The next morning at the battalion conference we were
told that we would be a motorised battalion working as
divisional troops and we were to pick up our transport of
some 87 vehicles on Imphal plain, now. Our total establish-

ment of trained drivers was twenty-four. We had twelve 15 cwt Chevrolets, one water tank mounted on a 15 cwt Ford chassis and two jeeps. Apart from the drivers there were some NCOs, VCOs and Officers who could drive. Since we had about six days in hand, training began at once, because if we could not man the vehicles we could not get to the start line – and so, at best would become line of communication troops! No, the 6/7th had to be there and preferably in front.

Our next shock came upon collection of the 87 vehicles. Though there were some 300 to 400 vehicles on the plains, few of them had any superstructures left. They were dirty and most badly damaged and upon enquiry we were told to pick our lot and go before anyone else came – and as an afterthought I was told that these were all vehicles whose 'lives' had finished in the North African campaign some two years previously and from the last push by West African troops down the Kabaw Valley! Everyone, from the CO to the most junior sepoy, was involved in making this mixed fleet of vehicles work. We needed every one of these vehicles to get the battalion to their start line and of course beyond. Our spares were very limited and did not necessarily fit every occasion or this conglomeration of makes and types. Beg, borrow or acquire were the orders and we had 96 hours. The Colonel, Jai Singh, and the writer did all major repairs. Shah Mohammed and Maneshwar Prasad Singh dealt with spare parts and without their efforts we could not have replaced things like batteries, half-shafts, sparking plugs, fuel pumps, dynamos and sundry nuts, bolts and tyres. The Colonel 'forgot' to ask who supplied our needs and I was too busy, and thankful that our task progressed satisfactorily.

It is very germane to mention here that those vehicles which had been with the West African forces were part of a campaign in 1944 that cleared the West Bank of the Irrawaddy of most Japanese forces, thus giving us, EXTENDED CAPITAL, an unopposed approach to the Irrawaddy. Because of this the CAPITAL campaign in the north having been launched earlier, most active enemy forces there had been drawn off north and thus away from our bridgehead. Our crossing by motorized landing craft, manned by the IASC, went smoothly, the timing of both thrusts, with the benefit of hindsight, was perfect. Our bridgehead was secured by the 7th Indian Division who cleared the actual crossing site at Nyaungu, south of Pakokku on 14 February 1945.

Meanwhile urgent driver training was going on. There was little or no sleep. At the appointed hour and day all vehicles were runners and manned and we reached the start line at Palel intact on the 3rd February with the loss of only one vehicle. For four nights and five days we followed the tank transporters and lorries through 2 to 3 ft of fine dust to the divisional concentration at Mynthe for the last minute adjustments and final briefings before we were on our way to the Irrawaddy some 5 miles away.

Officially we became the 17th Indian Division Recce Battalion, which hardly described our subsequent role. The order of battle of the infantry of our Division, emblem Black Cat, was as follows:

Plate 10: 17th Division Shoulder Flash –
Black Cat – worn by all ranks.

48th Indian Infantry Brigade	4/12th Frontier Force Regiment
	1/7th Gurkha Rifles
	1st West Yorkshire Regiment
63rd Indian Infantry Brigade	7/10th Baluch Regiment
	9th Border Regiment
	1/10th Gurkha Rifles
99th Indian Infantry Brigade	6/15th Punjab Regiment
	1st Sikh Light Infantry
	1/3rd Gurkha Rifles
Divisional Recce Battalion	6/7th Rajput Regiment
Divisional Defence Battalion	6/9th Jat Regiment
Divisional Machine Gun Battalion	9/13th Frontier Force Rifles

At Cynthe we were fortunate to make the acquaintance of Lieutenant Colonel W. Miron, the AQ of 17th Division who turned out to be a very good friend to the paltan in the days ahead.

Our approach drive to the Irrawaddy River, with our very mixed form of transport crammed with all our stores, petrol, kit and ammunition, was in itself a minor nightmare because we were ploughing through dust and loose sand created by our Sherman tanks and the transporters of 255th Tank Brigade who preceded us to Cynthe and the river. We just had to keep going.

One incident stands out to give some idea of the prevailing conditions. At night time we had limited visibility and headlights could not be used, only sidelights. The dust and sand seemed to be confined to a strip of some 8–10 ft in width. Our Dodge 6-wheelers were left hand drive and so the driver was nearest to the left hand edge of this 'dust track'. At night with the constant hum of the engines one of our vehicles thought they were on the right path. In actual fact the path should have been downward because it crossed a dried up riverbed. Quite suddenly the left hand side of the road went down whilst the right hand side went up! Everyone on board, some 20 soldiers, driver and NCOs and kit were ejected into the night as the vehicle turned over and fell on its back in the middle of the road! There were thankfully no casualties and the vehicle was turned over to rest on its wheels once more. The faithful Dodge engine restarted and we were on our way again. A lesson to stay awake!

We then made for Pauk and crossed the mighty Irrawaddy to be married up with Probyn's Horse (5th Lancers)[2] who were equipped with Sherman Tanks. We practised the 'drill' of climbing onto and dropping off the Shermans and trying the impossible, namely communicating with the individual tank commanders through their outside telephones affixed to the right rear track guard. With a bank of five Chrysler engines married to a single crankshaft turning over a few feet away there was little chance of either hearing or speaking. Probyn's Horse, realizing this difficulty, and to their eternal credit, stayed 'open' at all times. They lost many valuable tank commanders to snipers for the sake of good communications and our safety. Lieutenant Colonel Miles Smeeton was their CO and the two regiments spearheaded 17th Division's advance to Meiktila. In the relative flat and open country to Meiktila speed was not only essential, but also possible. The final load tables were completed and the battalion was organised as follows:

Tac HQ with Tank Regt HQ – 3 tanks (Tac HQ was the normal Recce group)

A Company Commander	Major S.H. Payne – With B Squadron Probyn's Horse
B Company Commander	Major B. Portugal –

---

[2] The 5th Lancers were from 255th Brigade and as such were part of IV Corps.

	With C Squadron Probyn's Horse
C Company Commander	Major G.R. Marriott – With A Squadron Probyn's Horse
D Company Commander	Major J. Cox – Truck Company for Recce purposes in 30 cwt Dodge Vehicles
A Echelon with Mortars	Under Command Lieutenant J. Knox
B Echelon	Captain K. Crossley, Lieutenant S.D.M. Ottowell and RMO – Lieutenant S.C. Sen IAMC

Meanwhile the Admin Box had been formed under the command of Captain J. Bateson and Lieutenant D.C.P. Blake. This remained with 17th Division's Admin Box at Cynthe and contained the majority of officers and men's kit. Therefore, the men went into action with only 6 lbs of kit. Large packs could not be taken for two reasons: sufficient transport was not available for carrying them, and it was impracticable to fight from tanks wearing large packs. The packs could not be left on tanks in action because of the likelihood of their catching fire and so endangering the tanks.

The afternoon before we set off we were all busy cleaning our weapons and arming our hand grenades, when we heard a loud explosion and Major Payne's orderly was tragically killed outright by the grenade he was arming. He was our first casualty.

The next day we were all introduced to a furious battle and casualties. As we set off from our Bridgehead we came across a heavily defended and bunkered village, Oyin and saw our very first action.

Oyin

Oyin was a very hard fought battle in which we discovered that the entire enemy had to be killed if we wished to stay alive and win, which we did, and laagered to the east of the village for the night. Darkness came down very quickly which did not allow us enough time to pick up all our wounded to bring them in. The next morning we realized that the local population had stripped all the dead, and if any were still alive, mercilessly killed them, for their clothing and any valuables.

Our introduction to war was brutal, without mercy, and sudden. The paltan's reaction was typical: they were not going to be beaten by the enemy's tactics. One such tactic used by Japanese snipers was to tie themselves to trees with branches, so they could fire on us even though wounded, and would continue to do so until killed. This usually meant that our Sherman tanks had to fire canister rounds and blow the sniper and half the tree away!

Our casualties, dead and wounded were approximately 70. Major Marriott and Jemadar Rang Khan, the Pioneer Jemadar, were killed and Major Portugal wounded. A count of enemy casualties, taken after we left, proved that Probyn's Horse and ourselves alone had accounted for 240 killed and it was estimated that the village had been held by at least 350 Japanese.

The next day we continued our way to Meiktila, about 50 miles down the road. Strung out on the road as we were, we were attacked by Zero fighter planes, but fortunately our air cover of Hurricanes and Spitfires put an end to that. Thereafter and throughout our advance, we were not molested by Japanese aircraft again. Our next objective was Maulaing. This place had been pounded very heavily by the Royal Air Force. We had an excellent set piece attack laid on, and took the place with no opposition except for the odd sniper. Harbouring that night some five miles beyond Maulaing we were for the first time subjected to a small attack on the perimeter. The attack was made by only a few enemy and came in on A Company's front. The following morning a dead Japanese officer was found a few yards from the wire and here we got our first Japanese sword. It was obviously a typical Japanese suicidal attack.

MEIKTILA

Our part in the plan for the attack on Meiktila was to conduct a sweep to the east and attack from east to west of the town using the railway line as an axis of advance. We met a few deserted Japanese positions just outside Meiktila, mostly anti-aircraft (AA) positions, and one or two AA LMGs were left behind. We arrived at the Kanda Railway Station without opposition and were just about to put our plans for the attack of Meiktila into operation when a hail of bullets came from south of the railway line. In addition the enemy began using electrical detonation devices to explode the petrol dumps.

The battalion continued to put its plan into operation. 'A' Company with tank support went into the attack along the north side of the railway whilst B Company started the advance along the south side, with the object of sweeping fairly wide and knocking out the Japanese strong point on the ridge some 250 yards to our south. 'A' Company made excellent progress and with very little opposition reached a point within sight of the Meiktila Railway Station.

For B Company the fight was furious and although they launched attack after attack upon the strong Japanese position they could not succeed in capturing it. C Company were then sent to attack the position from the rear, but before the attack was allowed to go in we were ordered by brigade to pull out because it was getting dark and it was necessary to go into harbour. The tanks quite obviously were not used at night. However, by then we had inflicted

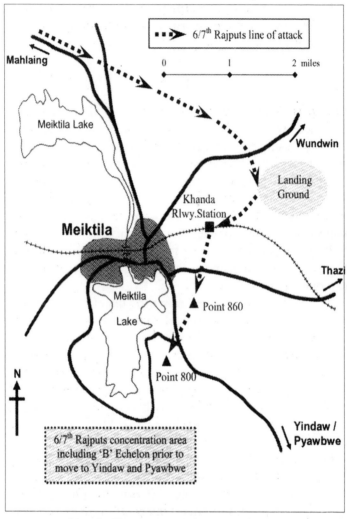

■ ■ ■ ➤ 6/7th Rajputs line of attack

Mahlaing

0   1   2 miles

Meiktila Lake

Wundwin

Landing
Ground

Khanda
Rlwy.Station

Meiktila

Thazi

Meiktila

Lake

Point 860

N

Point 800

Yindaw /
Pyawbwe

6/7th Rajputs concentration area
including 'B' Echelon prior to
move to Yindaw and Pyawbwe

Map 3: Sketch map of the battle for Meiktila
28 February–5 March 1945.

a lot of casualties upon the enemy and had almost cleared the strong point. To end the day, the tanks amused us with a shoot. They stood off from the position and poured dozens of 75 mm shells into it. The shoot was delightful to watch and I don't think any enemy were left when we evacuated.

As a point of interest eight MMGs were found in the enemy positions next morning and the ridge had a frontage of only about 200 yards. Our casualties amounted to approximately sixteen but still our men had their tails up, having, at that stage of the campaign, in conjunction with Probyn's Horse, accounted for several hundreds of the enemy for what were quite light casualties, especially in view of the fact that we were the attacking force. Probyn's Horse casualties were mainly to tank commanders who just refused to close down during any action. Undoubtedly their bravery was a magnificent encouragement to our men, who by this time had grown very fond of the tanks and their crews and could always count upon getting the fullest support.

The Divisional Commander appreciated that Meiktila was held in strength and laid on a very big set piece attack for the next day, supported by a considerable amount of artillery. We had only one company committed on this day, once again A Company, who were ordered to probe forward as much as possible on our original axis of advance, i.e. astride the railway, whilst another brigade was attacking the town from the south west.

Major Payne with his company competently carried out the task. They killed small parties of Japanese the whole way and eventually reached Pt 860 where a big pagoda was situated. There they met quite heavy opposition which they overcame and pushed further on to capture the road bridge over an inlet to the lake. This bridge was considered a vital point, and had been prepared for blowing by the Japanese.

During this action an amazing incident occurred. A

Japanese Officer rushed at the A Company Commander wielding his sword. Major Payne stood his ground firmly with bayonet fixed and waited. On pressing the trigger, however, he found to his horror he had forgotten to load, and the Japanese was then only a few yards away.

Major Payne decided on the bayonet, but the enemy sheered away from him and ran about a hundred yards into the middle of our men. He eventually fell, riddled with bullets. Thus the second sword was captured. A magnificent weapon it was, its former owner being a Battalion Commander of the rank of Major.

'A' Company pushed on to within sight of Pt 799 and late in the evening was given the order that Pt 860 and the bridge must be held at all costs. Major Payne considered it impossible to do this with only one company, and the CO on hearing this immediately asked permission to send another company, together with his Tactical HQ and essential Battalion HQ personnel, to hold Pt 860 and the bridge. This was granted and in support we were given the self propelled (SP) Battery and a very fine Observation Post (OP) up with us. The Japanese tried throughout the first night to get the bridge back, but with the aid of some excellent gunnery were held off. Further, it was obvious that the enemy was evacuating materials or stores from the cantonment area and the SP guns certainly 'did them over' throughout the night.

Next morning we were ordered to continue to hold the area as being a vital point whilst other attacks were going on in the west and south of the town. However there wasn't very much activity except for a terrific amount 'overs' from tank 75 mm Browning and other automatic fire as a result of the furious battle going on, on the other side of the lake. That night we again held our ground and the bridge and the only attack we were subjected to was one delivered on our Pt 860 box by what was obviously a suicide party. That was quickly stopped and we found a couple of dead enemy soldiers on the wire the next morning.

On this day RAF support obliged with a flight of Thunderbolts, which mistook the dug in platoon of C Company at the cross roads for Japanese! The Colonel in vain tried to stop them but our communications were via Division to the RAF and the action being so swift two more low level attacks were made before they broke it off. The platoon suffered about ten per cent casualties, but held their position. Thus we experienced 'Friendly Fire' for the first time.

A rescue mission was mounted but only got halfway there when it attracted Japanese fire from across their long front. John Knox, the mortar officer, was wounded through the back of his neck and generally speaking it was not a very healthy place to be. Now attached to our battalion was a 30 cwt ambulance truck donated by a ladies charity in the USA complete with a driver, also an American, by the name of George. He had been listed as 'unfit for active service' in the USA – a more willing and courageous individual and driver could not have existed. Having witnessed the attack at the crossroads he instantly requested permission to drive up the road to evacuate all casualties. So George broke all the rules of the Geneva Convention by loading the ambulance with the grenades and ammunition destined for C Company and promptly departed, sandwiched between two Sherman tanks, at full speed for the crossroads, whilst the rest awaited the ambulance's return and kept up a lively fire on the advancing Japanese who had, by then, been stopped. John Knox and C Company's casualties were flown out that afternoon from the airstrip, a part of which we still controlled.

We were unable to get our mortars through, but nevertheless Subedar Kedar Singh took his platoon into action with rifle and bayonet only and had a grand field day with no casualties. We continued to hold the vital points until 5 March and had several skirmishes with parties of the enemy.

However, on 5 March Meiktila was virtually clear and

the whole of the division moved into the town. The battalion had part of a box to defend and also Pt 799. The following day the airfield was better secured and so the rest of the battalion and the CO went to join A Company and Major Payne.

During our final stay in Meiktila we were kept in a reserve role for most of the time, as higher authorities decreed a rest, in spite of our representation to the contrary. We were allowed to send the odd platoon out on jobs with the tanks and certainly our truck company did a considerable amount of work and with several successes. We did manage to get the battalion out on show with Probyn's Horse, just to keep us in trim for the next round, but this only happened after we had reverted from division to tank brigade command. Incidentally during our short stay in Meiktila we were under command, at various times, of 17th Division, 48th Brigade, 99th Brigade, 9th Brigade of 5th Division, and 255th Tank Brigade. We feel this almost constitutes a record.

The fact that by this time we had collected many Japanese trophies including various automatic weapons, a couple of battalion guns, and last but by no means least an excellent staff car for 'Crazy' which hasn't so far been mentioned. The staff car was a great source of pre-occupation for the CO, who didn't take to the 'defensive role' too well.

This source of 'pre-occupation', the staff car, provided an interesting meeting. We had to clean the tank and all fuel lines – the Japanese had used paraffin – and decided to clean the engine and sump, which in due course was dropped. We were fixing it all back when quite suddenly some red tabs bent down to ask where our Colonel was. Not knowing the caller I asked him his name, whilst putting a nut on the top of a bolt which the Colonel was holding in position underneath the engine. I was told: that Colonel Armstrong wished to see my Colonel. Colonel Armstrong was a Staff Officer from IV Corps. The reply

I received through the engine was 'tell Effie I am busy'. I had no need to relay this to our visitor who then explained via the engine, that IV Corps wanted to know our exact location and perimeter at Meiktila. Reluctantly the Colonel came out, quite dirty, but unbowed with greasy hands and invited our visitor into his jeep and drove very fast around our perimeter returning with a somewhat shaken Staff Officer. On enquiry the Colonel explained 'Effie'[3] to me – it was not flattering.

From our bunkers overlooking the lake we discovered a large, steel-built open Ford three-tonner seemingly abandoned in a small field leading down to the lakeside. Through binoculars it appeared to be in good order so we decided to investigate. Fortunately this was done with the Colonel's knowledge. Jai Singh and the writer proceeded down the hillside to the field in question. We arrived and carefully checked the outside of the vehicle for any signs of booby traps or wires, but there were none. We opened the doors and to our delight found the keys in the ignition. This was all too good to be true. Suddenly the earth around us erupted and shells began arriving in the field with alarming rapidity. By then Jai Singh and I had split, we had been on opposite sides of the vehicle, and dived for the little cover, the few trees on either side, that the field afforded. What we did not know was that the Colonel had observed our progress and fortunately the Forward Observation Officer (FOO) happened to be there as well. The latter was instrumental in stopping the battery shelling the vehicle and the two of us. Now we both had personal experience of 'Friendly Fire'.

We managed to start the vehicle and very slowly drove it up the hill to our positions and onto some level ground. Further inspection showed that all four tyres were stuffed with grass, but the covers appeared to be in good condition. Driven on paraffin by the Japanese, it meant stripping and

[3] Colonel Armstrong's initials were E.F.

cleaning the carburettor, pumps and tank before filling up with petrol. The vehicle was renamed 'Meiktila Aggie' and as such stayed with us until the end of hostilities.

Meanwhile the Japanese high velocity 105mm and 150mm guns which had been shelling us were dealt with by Mitchell bombers, and the Japanese finally gave up allowing Meiktila to become itself again. We moved to the south of the town to prepare for our final 'drive' down the Rangoon Road.

Our B Echelon, QM and Subedar Major (SM) arrived from Cynthe with the bad news that all our stores and kit, personal or otherwise, had been bulldozed into a large grave on the orders of the Divisional B Echelon Commander and that all the hoped for clothing and MT spare parts were irrevocably buried. Frantic demands and excellent co-operation between units meant that we got everything ready for the next phase.

B Echelon also brought a further tale of woe: the Column Commander reported that a Burmese civilian had been killed by one of our vehicles. As MTO I had to get to the bottom of this story very quickly. The Division were being pressed by the civil administration, which was following up very closely behind 17th Division's advance. The vehicle number was given to us and it turned out to be a three-tonner in which, among others, the Subedar Major, Labh Singh, travelled! I knew the driver but could get no sense from him so as the SM must have been aware of something. I handed the whole matter over to the CO. It turned out later that for reasons known only to the SM, he was actually driving the three tonner at the time of the supposed incident!

This cast a momentary shadow over the 6/7th, which thankfully was soon dispersed by the urgency of our need to get ready for our advance south of Meiktila and subsequent battles. Sadly this whole incident could not be dealt with at once because of operational requirements and so was left in abeyance. A very unsatisfactory end leaving an alleged mishap open to many different interpretations – and we had only heard the worst without any proof. The whole problem arose out of 14th Army orders issued once we had entered Burma and the civil administration machinery moved in, in the wake of our successful advance. With the benefit of hindsight none of us really appreciated that civil administration meant civil law as well, which of course applied to areas no longer subject to the enemy's presence. Thus this whole episode, whilst coming as a shock to the SM, came as a surprise to us as well. The officers had just about heard enough tales of woe whilst sitting in a circle listening to our Quarter Master (QM), Captain Bateson, when suddenly without warning the QM let out a yell and leapt several feet into the air only to come down and dance frantically around whilst undoing his shorts to rid himself of the smouldering remains of a cigarette! An amusing end to a worrying day.

Three highly satisfactory events took place during our stay in Meiktila. The first was a personal complimentary message from the Divisional Commander congratulating the CO and the battalion on their fine work during the operations to date. Copy of the message is given below:

'02131 (.) RESTRICTED (.) PERSONAL TO HAYES NEWINGTON FROM DIV COMD (.) CONGRATULATE YOU ON YOUR LEADERSHIP AND YOUR BATTALION ON FINE FIGHTING SPIRIT SHOWN IN THEIR FIRST FIGHT (.) PROUD TO HAVE YOU UNDER COMMAND'.

Second, we met the 4th Battalion, who had come down from Jorhat to Meiktila with a brigade from the 5th Division.

And third we also received several immediate gallantry awards:

Lieutenant Colonel
   E.A. Hayes–Newington   Awarded the DSO
Major S.H. Payne   Awarded the MC
Subedar Chunni Singh   Awarded the MC
Jemadar Maldeo Singh   Awarded the MC
17609 L/Naik
   Raghubir Singh   Awarded the MM
34734 Sepoy Dal Singh   Awarded the MM

Plate 11: Patrols of the 6/7th Rajputs return from a search of
wooded country around Meiktila supported by
tanks of Probyn's Horse.

At this stage and particularly on our drive to Rangoon our main supply route was often too long and not protected from the enemy, so we frequently experienced air supply drops against our requirements given 12 hours before! It happened thus: our QM would inform AQ at Division of our detailed needs and Division passed this straight on to Air Supply at Corps HQ. It was a very fast service and we were never without petrol, ammunition, or basic rations. We in turn gave a map reference and marked out a 'safe' field.

With good heart we set off in company with Probyn's Horse to attack our next objective, Yindaw. The place was defended all round, except for the road entrance, by two earth walls into which they had, on the reverse sides, heavily defended bunkers so that they were mutually supporting. There were mines as well as an anti-tank measure.

CHAPTER 4

1945: The Scenic Route to Pyawbwe

We were warned for the second leg of the operation on or about 26 March, and briefly the Divisional plan was as follows:

The object was to attack and capture Pyawbwe and Yamethin to allow 5th Division to pass through and push down to Toungoo.

99th Brigade on foot were to secure Thazi and push down to Pyawbwe from the north. 63rd Brigade using the main Meiktila–Pyawbwe Road as an axis were to attack Pyawbwe from the east.

CLAUDCOL, commanded by Brigadier Pert DSO, Commander of 255 Tank Brigade, consisted of: Probyn's Horse with 6/7th Rajputs less C Company attached to the SP Battery and 7/10th Baluch; two companies of 4 Bombay Grenadiers and in support an SP Battery and other Divisional Artillery and Sappers, to sweep to the west, via Yindaw, Yanaung and Ywadan and cut the main Pyawbwe–Yamethin Road, prior to the combined assault on Pyawbwe.

YINDAW

CLAUDCOL moved from Meiktila early in the afternoon of 4 April. We harboured at a jumping off area a few miles south of Meiktila for the night of 4/5 April and were due off early next morning. Subsequently however, we were informed that the Border Regiment would attack with a view to capturing the village of Kalewa on the west side of road, and subject to this fairly big village being secured we would be required to put in an attack on Yindaw. We therefore moved off at 9.30 on the morning of 6 April, Brigade Tac HQ with Battalion Commanders in front, followed by the 6/7th Rajputs mounted on the tanks of Probyn's Horse.

By this time our company attachment with the tanks had changed slightly and we formed up with Probyn's Horse as follows:

A Company (OC Major S.H. Payne, MC) with A Squadron (OC Major Lorraine-Smith MC)

B Company (OC Major R.M. Hall vice Major Portugal wounded in Oyin on 22 February) with Truck and Recce Company.

C Company (OC Captain D.C.P. Blake vice Major G. Marriott killed in Oyin on 22 February) with Battery of SP Guns, as protection.

D Company (OC Major J. Cox with C Squadron (OC Major Arkinstall).

B Squadron Probyn's Horse was detached under Command 63rd Brigade.

We proceeded on the approach march and halted in a dispersal area near Wayindok, where the progress of the Borders was followed, it being vital that Kalewa be captured before our attack on Yindaw could go in. We received orders for our attack from the Brigade Commander at approximately 1.30 p.m., and a little later from the CO. The information was that Yindaw was held by up to 400 Japanese soldiers, plus five guns at the most. The attack was to be done in three phases. 'A' Company would complete the first phase, their objective being the road running from east to west 50 yards from the bund surrounding the village. Then D Company with artillery support was to secure the bund and form a bridgehead to

allow tanks, which could not negotiate either the moat or
the bund, to get into the village. Then the artillery and
B Company were to pass through and secure and hold the
southern end of the village.

We reached the start line after the code word *FOX* had
been given. *FOX*, by the way, signalled the success of the
attack by the Borders on the adjoining village of Kalewa
and the signal for our attack to begin. Good fun was had
by A Company supported by the tanks whilst still on the
start line, because some Japanese had decided to get out
of Kalewa and into Yindaw. They ran a considerable distance with tank Browning guns and our own chaps fairly
letting them have it. By this time our artillery had put
down the supporting fire, which for once was not up to its
usual very high standard of accuracy. We had quite a time
in Battalion HQ on this occasion because of 'Friendly Fire',
but fortunately we all managed to avoid the devastation of
the twenty-five pounders.

Off went A Company and after a little sniping, the
report came through from the Company Commander to
Battalion HQ, a hundred yards behind, that Phase One
was complete, the objective reached, and only two men
wounded. At the same time Major Payne asked, in view of
the fact that opposition had been light, to be allowed to
take the plan for the attack forward but the CO insisted
that the original plan should be adhered to. Hence Phase
Two, the bridgehead phase, was put into action. It had not
developed very far when we met some of the overshoots
from our own artillery.

It is necessary to pause a few moments before continuing
the narrative to give some small description of what Yindaw
was like from the stand point of both the attackers and the
defenders. The village was quite dense with many well-
constructed Burmese houses and *bashas*.[1] The length of
the village was about 600 yards and the width 500 yards.

---

[1] Temporary accommodation of a tent like structure not enclosed.

Surrounding it was a considerable moat followed by an embankment 12 to 15 ft in height. There were two roads leading through the village, one the main road to Pyawbwe, and the other some 200 yards further east and parallel to the first. It was this last which carried the bridge across the bund and moat, and making it obvious why we had to establish a bridgehead for the tanks. Incidentally, the moat which contained a fair amount of water, which had to be negotiated before the bund could be reached. To sum up, the village was the finest defence position conceivable, surrounded by a perfect tank obstacle – so that, holding the bund with good fields of fire gave every advantage to the defence.

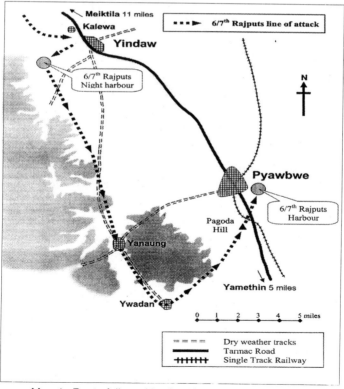

Map 4: Route followed by the 6/7th Rajputs to Pyawbwe.

D Company moved forward and came under heavy automatic fire which covered the moat, but in spite of this, and by getting across the moat at good speed, only a few casualties were incurred. As was to be expected, D Company met considerable opposition from the bund and behind it, but once again by a determined attack they rushed up and over and proceeded to systematically wipe out the first line of defence with grenades and everything else they could use.

This first line of defence was quite strongly held, but not as one anticipated in small positions. On the contrary, the defences consisted of large twenty-man bunkers which, once they were bypassed, were not so difficult to destroy from the rear, including their occupants. Only to the right was the battle at all sticky and as Battalion HQ had reached the top of the bund by this time, the CO had a few words with Major Cox, the Company Commander, and suggested that if the right hand platoon went still further to the right it might be possible to infiltrate through. The Company Commander duly adopted this plan and D Company moved forward to what proved to be the second line of defence. Here the fighting was fierce and continued for well over an hour, and although progress was made and casualties inflicted upon the enemy they were at the expense of heavy casualties to ourselves. Moreover the bridgehead was still not properly established, because as soon as the leading tank reached the bridge, artillery, heavy mortar and grenade discharger fire was put down on the mined bridge, making it very difficult for the sappers to lift the mines for the tanks to pass.

It was in this fierce fighting that we suffered our second fatal casualty amongst the British officers. Major Cox was killed whilst gallantly leading his company in the action described above. The loss of such a fine officer was a very hard blow and he was deeply mourned by all ranks.

The Sapper Lieutenant was magnificent throughout the battle, and how he escaped is a miracle of fate. He succeeded in clearing many mines from the bridge, but his efforts like ours still failed to let the tanks get in. B Company was now brought up to reinforce D Company, already getting numerically weak through casualties, and the action continued fiercely. Battalion HQ came under fairly heavy sniper and automatic fire and had to come down off the bund. We hoped to move further right to watch the activities of the right hand platoon, who were battling it out in fairly dense surroundings. However, no sooner had we come off the bund, a very exposed position, than a Japanese soldier rolled a grenade down into the middle of us. It rather goes to prove the ineffectiveness of the Japanese grenade, for all that happened was that the Adjutant's Orderly, a veteran called Iqbal, sustained a badly cut arm. After this, we changed our position to some twenty yards further down the bund.

At approximately 5.45 p.m. the Brigade Commander ordered the battalion to pull out of the battle, owing to coming darkness and the undesirability of operating tanks after dark. The CO gave orders to evacuate all casualties under covering fire from B Company and many excellent efforts to complete the task were made by all ranks, in the face of heavy enemy fire. Most of the casualties were brought safely back, but in trying to get back the more forward ones, we were sustaining further losses. The body of Major Cox could not be recovered. His heroism in the leadership of his Company can seldom be surpassed, his body being one of those far forward amidst the enemy positions. In the event a pullout was organized in laybacks with support from the tanks and went according to plan.

The men had had a very hard day but in spite of the fact that the attack was unsuccessful, and that we had sustained in the region of seventy casualties, they were in good heart. They thought, at any rate, the Japanese had paid very expensively for having taken us to task at Yindaw. Amongst the casualties, in addition to Major Cox killed, were Major Crossley missing, and Subedar Rahmat Ali (the latest VCO arrival) who was killed after acquitting himself excellently. He was known through the Rajput Regiment as the *sab se bari munchh wala*.[2]

The Japanese were respected for their ability with camouflage and the building of defences and Yindaw, which by its geography lent itself to defence, was made into the finest defensive position the battalion ever encountered during the whole campaign. It is interesting to recall that our Subedar Major Labh Singh, visited the village some weeks after the action and saw the following defences. 'There were five lines of large bunker positions running from east to west of the village. Each bunker was built to hold twenty or thirty men. In addition there were smaller positions excellently sited and camouflaged. From the southern end of the village a large underground tunnel had been made, which according to local reports ran a mile or two from the village and out into jungle country'.

It is interesting to note that we now understand that at about the time of our attack, General Honda was very likely passing through and out of Yindaw via the underground tunnel to Pyawbwe to catch up with the remnants of his Japanese 33rd Army. The enemy no doubt made very good use of this method of escape when, for five days, a large proportion of divisional artillery pounded the place and considerable air strikes by Mitchells, Thunderbolts and Hurribombers were made. The village was flattened, but quite a number of bunker positions remained intact.

PAGODA HILL

On the following day we by-passed Yindaw and harboured a few miles to the south-west for one day prior to moving on to our next objective, Yanaung.

We were not the leading troops for the first 6 miles or so, as the Bombay Grenadiers wanted their turn. Things

[2] The man with the biggest moustache.

were a bit sticky for there were some nasty nullahs to cross, for some of which tanks had to make considerable recces. We reached the area of Widin, where Subedar Maldeo Singh[3] MC, with a platoon (from A Company), was sent to clear through some very dense country to the east, from which direction there had been quite a lot of nuisance value sniping. It was here that we got the first Prisoner of War we had ever seen, although we were to see many afterwards, but not in such good condition. Incidentally the men were not at all happy to take a prisoner, but we were told that the 'I Chiefs'[4] wanted one occasionally, so he was preserved from harm.

On 8 April we again took over as forward troops with, of course, our very firm friends Probyn's Horse. We cracked away to an early start with the same objective as the previous day, Yanaung, and we arrived there at about breakfast time. We had little information as to what we were likely to meet there, but took a broad view and decided against 'time spent in recce' and in favour of a short sharp attack, before the enemy had rid their eyes of sleep. Once again there was a bund, but only on the west and northern flanks, with another running from north to south and meeting the junction of the first two. We had planned what may be the hard way, but at least the way by which we should be sure to find the enemy, for we had by this time realized that he always held embankments and bunds.

One platoon of A Company with one troop of tanks was pushed forward to get along the bund to the north-west junction and thence to push forward to the south-west corner. Another platoon, following close behind, was to turn east at the junction and capture the length of the north bund. One platoon of D Company with a squadron of tanks were at the same time to make a wide sweep to

[3] Promoted since Meiktila.
[4] Intelligence Chiefs

the south-west corner of the bund and come into the village from the south-west.

As we had anticipated, the bund was very strongly held, but without doubt we had beaten the Japanese this time for they had not expected us to push along the top of the fairly wide bund. In addition we had some excellent mortar fire on the north bund and in the nullah just before it, which did extraordinary damage to the enemy. It turned out to be a real *shikar*[5] and in all that day, or at least by midday, we had a further two hundred Japanese to our score, with our own casualties one killed and ten wounded. If Yindaw had set our tails back in some small degree then Yanaung could only be described as providential, for the men were keen to crack on all night and find some Japanese, but we had to 'harbour'[6] at the 12½ milestone from Yamethin.

As further proof of the splendid co-operation we had with Probyn's Horse, the CO of that Regiment, Colonel Miles Smeeton, ordered that in view of the fact that we had taken a nasty knock at Yindaw, when the tanks could do little to help us, we should if possible, not have a single casualty on this day. The tanks and tank commanders should take no risk. As will be seen, our casualties could scarcely have been lighter and credit must go to the excellent work of the tanks, and incidentally to our own battalion mortars with, under command, five mortars belonging to the Bombay Grenadiers. Subedar Kedar Singh, in the absence of Lieutenant Knox, wounded at Meiktila, commanded the mortar fire support so well that the tanks asked for more of it than did our own infantrymen. They loved it and we used far more bombs in three hours than we had used in the whole campaign to date, admittedly mainly due to the best opportunity we had of

[5] Chase.
[6] A harbour is a temporary defended position from all points of the compass, usually set up for a night halt or in preparation for a move to another start line for further action.

using our own support. Incidentally this day was the CO's birthday and Colonel Smeeton and the CO had hoped to have a good killing – we did!

We now drove across country avoiding the 'road' and it being the dry season the nullahs and fields offered a fine surface for our tanks and vehicles. Thus we by-passed Yindaw and Pyawbwe and were on our way to Ywadan when suddenly the last four Rajput vehicles in the convoy were fired upon. A bullet passing very close over the driver's head, and through the seating anatomy of our Jemadar Quarter Master sitting on his stores in the back of the vehicle. The convoy came to a halt. Jai Singh, who was travelling with me in the last vehicle in the Rajput convoy, immediately jumped into the vacant driver's seat to try to restart the convoy but his action only brought forth more bullets. We had no means of knowing what the strength of the opposition was and being a 'soft vehicle' convoy the best we could do was to defend ourselves, i.e. the drivers and QM personnel. Fortunately at the rear of the convoy was a platoon from the Bombay Grenadiers who helped us guard our front, which seemed to be the part that the enemy wished to attack.

The night was very dark, there was little or no moon, but at least the sky was light enough to enable us to distinguish between bushes and trees. Our farrier L/Duffadar Haider Khan, a veteran of Gallipoli in the 1914–18 War, was very alert and requested permission to go to a small clump of trees with his rifle and his two bandoleers of ammunition, because he felt he would be outflanking the enemy's efforts to pass round our front. We had by this time assessed that the enemy was a fighting patrol of about platoon strength and, for some reason we could not understand, they did not attack the line of soft vehicles at their mercy but did everything to try and pass our front. Haider Khan required no assistance and departed silently into the night towards his objective. At moments during the night and in the early morning odd shots would come from the little copse on our right and we knew Haider Khan was defending himself, and some Japanese dead were found on our front, to the right, in daylight.

But daylight also revealed the true reason for the whole operation – the trees to the right of our advance and the copse to which Haider Khan had gone concealed trap doors covering bunkers containing much Japanese reserve ammunition. In view of their plight at Pyawbwe, they needed this very badly, so quite unwittingly, we had denied them this and all their storage facilities in the region of the head of the convoy, where we were ambushed! Haider Khan rejoined us as soon as a fighting patrol swept their way towards us from the battalion's position some 2 miles further, which we reached in time for a quick *chhota hazri*[7] and then the advance continued to Pagoda Hill via Ywadan. En route we found much disorder among the enemy who was retiring – not always fast enough.

Crossing a very wide nullah most of the battalion witnessed a remarkable feat by the CO. At about 600 yards a Japanese soldier was seen running across the nullah. The Colonel was standing on a tank and with his rifle killed the enemy with a single shot. I should explain that officers and VCOs by now used rifles rather than sten guns or revolvers. We were travelling through much dust all day and the latter would not always work or at best were inaccurate, whereas the rifle always functioned and was accurate, in any case at 600 yards the enemy would have been safe from Stengun fire!

We knocked the enemy out of Ywadan and cleared through to the *chaung*[8] to the south, whilst D Company took on the villages on the other side. As soon as D Company with its squadron had crossed the *chaung* and into the opposite villages, the enemy started running out to make their escape down the nullah westwards.

[7] Little breakfast.
[8] Dry riverbed.

However, we were hoping that this would happen, for Battalion HQ, with Tank Brigade Tac HQ, were beautifully placed to deal with the situation. Heaven knows who shot which Japanese, but we all claimed each one as they ran out. Perhaps this was not good conservation of ammunition, but the excitement was so great that we didn't discourage the men from testing their rifles, not for some little time at any rate, until we thought fire discipline should be brought to bear. Having cleared these villages, and having bagged at least a hundred of our enemy, we turned due east and made rapid progress towards the Pyawbwe–Yamethin Road. We reached it at approximately 8 miles to the north of Yamethin.

The CO was then ordered to recce the Night Harbour area, but did not like the site suggested. Instead he decided to take a risk by going on to Pagoda Hill a good artillery target, but affording an excellent shoot all round and especially of the road in front for at least a mile. Here we expected to find some Japanese traffic pulling out of Pyawbwe, or supplying that place from Yamethin and we therefore organized a roadblock, sited in relation to our position.

Tanks and SP guns faced the road, with infantry protection all round, whilst the rear of the box was protected mainly by infantry, with a few tanks and armoured cars. As already mentioned, the battalion organized a 'roadblock' but, owing partly to the late arrival of troops in the harbour, our men were only just going into position when the evening party started. Soon after dark a fairly long convoy was seen approaching from the Yamethin direction, at approximately a mile from the harbour area. The convoy was excellently spaced; every vehicle had headlights full on, and consisted of various types of lorries, about a dozen in all. Everyone remained silent until the first lorry had passed the harbour and proceeded about 200 yards on. By this time we had the whole convoy lined up in front of us and the signal went up to open fire. I think most of

the tank 75 mm and Brownings fired for the kill, as did
D Company, who were very well placed. The sight was
amazing, very quickly after the 'open fire' all headlights
were turned off, but it was too late. The majority of that
Japanese convoy finished up in a sorry mess. Defensive
fire (DF) was laid on at what was considered the appro-
priate time when vehicles which got through would be
passing, and the result next morning proved the fire
effective, for a further three lorries were found on the DF
Spot, all in a derelict condition.

The Japanese in Pyawbwe too, seemed oblivious to our
presence on Pagoda Hill, because at about midnight a
further convoy was observed coming from the direction
of Pyawbwe and this time the prize was worthwhile for at
least three tanks were included in the convoy. Once again
our tank seventy fives and SP gunners had their money's
worth, with the result that three tanks were knocked out,
without a hope of retaliation, including one which sheered
off the road in time, only to meet our tanks in the rear of
the perimeter. Altogether our bag of Japanese MT had
been pretty good for the day, for prior to going into
harbour, an MT park was discovered with no one to guard
it. Tommy gun and pistol fire managed to wreck each
engine in turn, it became a question of who should open
the bonnet and who should fire into the more technical
parts of the engine. About twenty vehicles were accounted
for in this manner. Casualties for 9 April were over one
hundred enemy. Our own casualties were 3 killed and 19
wounded.

So far throughout the advance from the Irrawaddy we
had been operating in open country, dry and hot during
the day and only a little cooler at night. The battalion
naturally depended on receiving daily fresh drinkable
water. Our enemy made sure that much of this life giving
fluid was withheld by poisoning many wells on our route.
Our water-carrier was a Ford four wheel drive 30 cwt with
a water tank mounted. Probably the most important

vehicle in the battalion with the benefit of hindsight. Our dependence on it was absolute. Naik Mubarik Ali, the water tank driver, used to turn up tired but cheerful and rejoin the convoy towards our night's laager and always with his tank full to the brim with drinkable water. All water quality was tested before the tank was filled. Throughout the campaign, and wherever we were, we always had fresh water and in the hot weather of central Burma this was a vital need of the paltan.

PYAWBWE

10 April was spent in an advance up the Yamethin–Pyawbwe Road towards our objective. We had cleared several villages on the way and found some large Japanese dumps, a number of staff cars and a few more tanks, all with sleeping crews who hadn't time to wake up. We imagined big prizes for the capture of Mindan, a village about 2 miles from Pyawbwe, in which it was thought a Japanese HQ was established. There may have been but they certainly hadn't waited for D Company who cleared through it. Dumps and other structures rather indicated that this assumption was correct however, and further to substantiate that belief, it is probable that the staff cars that we found abandoned were originally for the senior officers of that HQ.

We arrived a few hundred yards from Pyawbwe, which by this time was being attacked from the west by 63rd Brigade and a squadron of Probyn's Horse, whilst 48th Brigade and 99th Brigade were coming in from their respective flanks. It was decided that we should not attack at such a late hour of the day: the sun was setting, and there appeared to be quite a number of Japanese running in all directions just inside the town. Therefore the tanks and infantry stayed off and enjoyed some good shooting at the obviously bewildered enemy.

We formed our perimeter a mile or so to the south of

the town ready for the next day's attack and by this time the Border Regiment of 63rd Brigade had captured and secured the railway station and the part of the town to the west before the station. We had a small attack on our perimeter that night, on C Company's front, probably a suicide party, and unfortunately our armourer (attached) was wounded and had to be evacuated.

At six the following morning the CO was called to Brigade HQ for a conference regarding the attack on Pyawbwe. He was to be in command of the whole party, including Royal Engineers and tanks. A sapper detachment was very necessary as it was believed that the approaches to the town had been heavily mined, although somewhat hastily.

The CO gave out his orders for an attack at 6.15 a.m. the next day. He decided that tanks would not be used, but that we should do the job in short bounds to allow the sappers to come up under our protection and clear a pathway through the mines for the tanks to come in behind us. It meant a probably hard task for the battalion, but although given a free hand with the use of his tanks, the CO would not risk one of them. His decision was greatly appreciated by their Regimental Commander Colonel Smeeton. Had he been asked he would have taken any risk to support us.

As for the capture of Pyawbwe, we started very well. The attack was staged in three phases, two to be done by our battalion and the third by a company from another battalion, put under our command for this particular action.

The first phase was completed in twenty minutes. We met no opposition but thirty Japanese bodies were counted and C Company, now under command of Captain Blake, found one Bren gun and a 105 mm gun, the latter in perfect condition. We couldn't get it out or the training centre might have had a further very good trophy. The Adjutant reported to the Brigade Commander that the Phase 1 had been completed and that with his permission we would continue Phase 3 simultaneously with Phase 2, despite the fact that the other company were not yet in position to carry out their task. We also arranged protection for the sappers who had a few mines to clear away before the tanks could come along. Our Phase 2 was proceeding very well with Major S.H. Payne MC in command, because the CO was confident after the initial success that we would not meet many Japanese and it gave Harry Payne a good chance to lead the battalion with the CO as onlooker.

The battalion made rapid progress, but we became worried when we realized that our right flank troops, who were to complete Phase 2, had not so far appeared. We thus consolidated our position, extended D Company plus the defence platoon over our two company front, and despatched C Company to fill the gap. That company met only one or two of the enemy, who offered no resistance

(IWM SE3773)

Plate 12: The 6/7th Rajputs clearing Pyawbwe.

being too tired to fight. We also captured another 75 mm gun. As soon as C Company reached their phase line the battalion proceeded on a very wide front to complete both Phases 2 and 3 and cleared through the main area of the town. We rejoiced in having no casualties and were satisfied that we had cleaned up in the area. Only half a dozen live enemy being found.

It was now 5th Division's turn to take the lead in the advance and plans were made for a short breather for 17th Division and part of 255th Tank Brigade, including Probyn's Horse. We ourselves reverted to divisional command and settled in Pyawbwe for a few days, doing defence work for the box and a morning parade of drill, physical training, and some weapon training. Major General Cowan visited the battalion and congratulated the VCOs and men upon their good show to date. The officers met the General at a separate meeting.

CHAPTER 5

1945: Advance towards Rangoon

On 13 April, the CO received orders that the battalion should advance immediately to Yamethin, and carry out a relief in place.

It will be remembered that part of CLAUDCOL had already visited Yamethin and in point of fact the Border Regiment stayed there for tea. They met no opposition however, as the Japanese were not interested in a battle at that stage. Subsequently, owing to a lack of troops, that part of CLAUDCOL had to rejoin its parent force and when 5th Division took the capture of the place as their orders directed, the Japanese pulled a very cunning move. Most of the town they left undefended allowing the tanks to go through in the belief that there were no Japanese present, especially as part of CLAUDCOL had already been there and met no opposition. However, a British battalion which followed after the tanks, were ambushed when the Japanese came in from each side of the town and attacked them from either flank. In the event it proved very difficult to rescue them. As a result of the foregoing it was not until the evening of 16 April that we ourselves reached Yamethin and took over its defence.

Whilst this was happening 5th Division and another column from 255th Tank Brigade known as SMEECOL, commanded by Colonel Smeeton and consisting of Probyn's Horse and a battalion of infantry, continued the push down the road. Their objective was to capture Toungoo

and Pyu, from where 17th Division would again take over
as forward troops from 5th Division.

We were still to continue in our role of tank infantry,
but this time we were to be paired with the Royal Deccan
Horse (9th Cavalry) and take over the role of 'leading
troops' from Pyu. In the meantime we continued to follow
up 5th Division ready to take over. On 25 April we started
the take over and the Battalion lined up with the tanks as
follows:

A Company with C Squadron Royal Deccan Horse.

B Company with B Squadron Royal Deccan Horse.

C Company with A Squadron Royal Deccan Horse.

D Company were now teamed up with the SP Guns, having taken
over from C Company.

As D Company retained the trucks for their own use
we had to get our Headquarters staff onto what tanks were
available in the three squadrons. The Mortar Platoon was
left behind at Tatkon, south of Yamethin, awaiting transport to bring them up to join the battalion. Our Headquarters were therefore split up, except of course Tac HQ
and the snipers who still travelled on regimental HQ tanks.
The Pioneer platoon travelled with A Company and the
Defence platoon and supernumeraries from Headquarters
with B and C Companies.

It was about here when we were sitting by the roadside
and we had eaten a hasty meal that a jeep with driver and
a civilian passenger drew up. The latter got out and came
over to our Colonel. The dialogue went something like
this: *'My name's Wagg, Hearst Press!' The Colonel thinking
that the man's nickname was 'Wag', replied 'Mine's Crazy'.*

They got on like a house on fire and instead of writing
us up he stayed with his jeep and helped for the next two
days with the evacuation of our casualties. The man in
question was in fact Alfred Wagg, the American author

and journalist. He had by then visited many theatres of war but, he was astonished by the cool, calm behaviour and sheer professionalism of the 6/7th, which he had not met before and had every admiration for us – so he decided to help us where he could by way of a 'thank you'.

We advanced from Pyu and reached the nullah just to the south; this was quite difficult to negotiate but a recce proved fruitful and there we encountered the first Japanese, only a small party, in the village of Leikdi but with some artillery pieces. That opposition was cleared up very quickly and we duly found their three guns. By 7.15 p.m. the same evening we reached Kanyutkwin, not great progress, but we had difficulty in getting across the river Pyu. Indeed part of the battalion arrived around midnight whilst A Company were left out all night to guard a scissors bridge, erected over a broken wooden bridge.

The CO then went to Brigade HQ for orders for the move down the road for the next day, 26 April. His orders were to establish contact with the enemy if possible and clear through as far as Nyaunglebin MS 96.[1] By reason of A Company's absence it was decided that they should be reserve company and follow with A Echelon, whilst the Company Commander would chase up and meet at the 'Orders Group'. Tac HQ with the 'Orders Group' and wireless communication advanced from Kanyutkwin at 5.30 a.m. on 26 April. We had forsaken tanks for jeeps, with the advantage of their being more convenient for Recce, especially as we had the Deccan Horse Recce troop out in front also. The Second-in-Commands of squadrons and companies brought their troops along quite close to the rear of Tac HQ, before we moved off again.

Penwegon, MS 122 was reported clear at 6.10 a.m., Kyauktaga MS 115 at 7.05 a.m., and Peinzalko MS 108 at 8.20 a.m., so the advance was making good progress. Beyond Peinzalko we advanced towards MS 100, meeting

[1] Milestone with distance from Rangoon in miles.

very slight opposition. The few enemy there proved to be terribly disorganized, preferring to run in all directions as we approached. They thus were no nuisance at all and were soon dealt with by Captain Blake and his merry men.

Whilst this was happening, A Company, who were bringing up the rear of the column, had news of some enemy in a village near MS 107. As they moved in with their tanks, the enemy moved out at the double southwards down the railway line leaving many mules behind. However, the tanks and infantry made better speed in pursuit and accounted for about eighty Japanese with no loss to themselves. Battalion HQ couldn't be kept out of it either, for whilst C Company were clearing up to MS 99, we were watching progress when, much to our amazement, what appeared to be some hundred enemy were seen moving along the railway line, and approaching our east flank. They too must have got the news that we were on the way and had decided to make a dash for safety. Their safety, unfortunately for them, resembled dummy targets for the SP gunners, OP tank and regiment HQ tanks. It is difficult to say how many Japanese appeared for the benefit of Battalion HQ, and were killed, because we hadn't the time to stop and mop up, especially as it was obvious that they were in bad physical condition and were concerned only with getting away.

It is interesting to note that at this time the sight of the enemy was becoming frequent, so much so that we were prepared to ignore the odd few. Even a most miserable specimen that came out from the hedges desirous of being taken prisoner was ignored. We managed to persuade him to continue walking in the opposite direction from our axis of advance, and expressed the hope that someone in the rear might take a more lenient view and pick him up. What a contrast from those Japanese we had met in all of our actions up to the time of Pyawbwe!

At five past ten in the morning our advance elements reached Bund BLACK, which was our objective at Nyaunglebin, although there was nothing there, except some railway wagons and stores of rice on fire. One railway wagon must have been loaded with fairly heavy ammunition, for pieces of shrapnel whizzed through the air, but fortunately very high up. C Company reported Nyaunglebin clear half an hour later, and we were told to consolidate and await further orders.

Further orders were given at noon after the CO met the Brigadier at Brigade Tac HQ and we were given the order to proceed with our tank friends to Pyuntaza MS 92. Thence to seize and hold the Yenwe Ghaung bridge at MS 90 until relieved by the Gurkhas soon afterwards. We then took a little time off for a 'brew up' and some cheese and biscuits and waited anxiously for the next orders, which turned out to be a 'harbour' for the night. These orders were received at approximately eight in the evening and we duly harboured, happy with the day's deeds and even more relieved at going into harbour at such an early hour. Additionally, with the excellent prospect of Bateson and Ottowell arriving with the Echelons, which of course meant *khana*[2] and if they arrived in good time, a nicely cooked dinner.

Mentioning a nicely cooked meal reminds one that at least a few words of praise must be given to the then L/Naik later Havildar Harbaksh Singh, the Mess Havildar. He and his staff certainly produced a good feed at any hour, night as well as day, and further with the aid of 'Meiktila Aggie', the captured Japanese lorry, always managed to fix us up with shelter from the rain, a table, chairs, and all the comforts of a field mess. The radio was always functioning, so we were able to keep abreast with events in Europe in spite of receiving few newspapers.

The next set of orders, given by Brigade for the continuation of the attack, were very bold, but perhaps justifiably so in view of the fact that during the last 100 miles,

[2] Food.

the opposition had been negligible. Perhaps they too were guided by a strong desire to reach Rangoon as early as possible.

Rangoon was seen as the prize of prizes; more important, we wanted to capture Rangoon before the monsoon began.[3] The rains would put the tanks virtually out of action, they being unable to leave the road once the paddy fields really began to get soaked. A third reason for haste, and this also was very important to 'Punch' Cowan and his 17th Division, lay in the fact that we had a shrewd idea that both 5th Division and 19th Division were keen on getting to Rangoon first. 5th Division were insistent that we had had our share and that it was now their turn to take the lead, whilst 19th Division kept sending advanced elements of their division to steal past our leading armour when in night harbour! Indeed both 17th and 19th Divisions were accused, perhaps justifiably, of establishing road blocks for each other, 17th to prevent anyone getting in front during the hours of darkness and 19th, having succeeded in getting somebody out in front, to hold us up the next day.

Pyinbongyi and Payagale

Our orders were to advance to Pegu. Information about the enemy was sparse and it was decided that we should continue our policy of clearing down the main road and destroying the enemy wherever met. To assist, we had a squadron of 7th Cavalry with armoured cars and Stuart tanks. The order of march was 7th Cavalry, B Company, Tac HQ, C Company, A Company and Echelons. Each rifle company was mounted on tanks. Start time was 5.30 a.m.

The advance guard moved off at the appointed hour

[3] The weather had been dry during the advance south from the Irrawaddy River.

and it wasn't until 10.30 a.m., when we reached Taxon MS 70, that we contacted any enemy – the opposition consisted of snipers and tank hunting parties. B Company cleared through the village and consolidated on the southern edge whilst C Company moved through and became the leading troops with 7th Cavalry. Only a few hundred yards more had been covered when we received information from the leading light tanks that they had been fired upon fairly heavily by automatics from Pyinbongyi village MS 69. This report was received at 1.30 p.m. In addition to the automatic fire, the Light Cavalry located a Japanese tank, dug in and being used in a static role. The 7th Cavalry did an excellent job in putting the tank out of action whilst plans were being made for the attack on Pyinbongyi.

Enemy tactics at this time followed the principle of placing sniper screens well ahead of their main positions. These were suicide squads, and the Japanese always employed such tactics. The fact that they were holding Pyinbongyi and other main villages on the road to Pegu definitely suggested that they were anxious to hold up our advance whilst they evacuated places such as Pegu and Rangoon; indeed already we had received local information that Rangoon was being evacuated. A frontal attack was now planned, with 7th Cavalry moving round to the east to protect the left flank of our troops, as there were several small villages out to the east of Pyinbongyi.

At Pyinbongyi the railway runs parallel with the road and 200 yards to the west. So the plan was for C Company to attack to the right of our axis, followed by B Company to do the mopping up, and one company of 1/3rd Gurkhas to put in a simultaneous attack on the left side of the village. The C Company boundary included the road and railway. B Company were to follow C Company as we considered the main danger would come from the railway bund, which, as was always the case with railway embankments, was held strongly. We started with five minutes of artillery fire on the northern end of the village and the SP gunners put down a considerable amount of airburst for five minutes.

Whilst the artillery fire was going down, C Company with its tank support advanced from the start line, 400 yards from the northern edge of the village. The ground was very soggy and 200 yards from the village one tank became stuck, and the remainder hadn't gone very much further when they too were in danger of becoming bogged down. It was therefore decided that the tanks would have to move back and enter the village via the road in order to link up with the infantry who would continue the advance into the village.

The railway embankment and station were held very strongly with quite a number of bunker positions; but in spite of no tank support C Company pushed through to make the first bound, which was the nullah running from east to west through the village, by 3.30 p.m. To the left of the village, only small enemy sniping was encountered, and the Gurkhas secured their same bound a little earlier than C Company.

The tanks in the meantime had managed to get into the village, but not before the loss of the bulldozer tank, which was in action for the first time, and the loss of one more tank, both blown up by electrically detonated mines. At this stage of the battle, the forward troops were told to consolidate the first bound and await the arrival of the tanks before proceeding onto the second and last bound, which would take them beyond the southern limit of the village and out into the open. At 3.45 p.m. the tanks joined the infantry and the attack again developed for completion of the second bounds.

The second half of the battle for Pyinbongyi proved a tougher nut to crack than had the first and at one particular point we incurred quite a number of casualties, including Jemadar Ram Singh who was sadly killed. The casualties all resulted from a fairly large bunker position, sighted on the railway bund 50 yards from the end of the first bound. These Japanese had remained very silent even whilst we were consolidating our first bound. By half past four in the afternoon C Company Commander reported that the objective had been secured and consolidation was taking place. In the meantime B Company went through on

Plate 13: A tank bogged down soon after the advance had begun. The dense smoke was caused by a grenade explosion, which set alight a large wooden house containing a Japanese ammunition store.

Plate 14: First stage of the advance with the artillery still firing. Three airbursts can be seen above the trees. The troops in the picture were the right hand platoon of C Company the 6/7th Rajputs.

Plate 15: The battle well under way. The soldier in the foreground watching for enemy with polecharges – during this lull the route into the village was being cleared of mines. There were always two men per tank for protection.

Plate 16: Tanks moving into the village with the 6/7th Rajput escort.

C Company's front and dealt with the few Japanese who had been missed.

Casualties to the enemy that day were estimated at 65 killed. These were actually counted whilst further reports put the figure at almost double. Our own casualties were five killed and twelve wounded. C Company had most certainly done a very fine job and for the most part, without tank support which was made difficult by the unsuitable terrain. For the attack on Pyinbongyi we had a press photographer and a reporter with us and the photographs at Plates 13–16 appeared later in *Fauji Akhbar*.[4]

To continue the action at Pyinbongyi, C and B Companies were relieved by the three remaining companies of 1/3rd Gurkhas, who held the village for the night. The tank brigade harbour was established at MS 69½ .

The next day saw one of the fiercest actions the battalion had yet fought. We were ordered to continue the advance on 29 April and 7th Cavalry were again in the lead closely followed by A Company on tanks, then Tac HQ, and C and B Companies respectively. The enemy was encountered, after an advance of only four miles, at Wunb-In, and once again we ran into the sniper screen, as was the case before the action of the previous day at Pyinbongyi. 'A' Company, led by Major Payne, quickly dealt with the screen, but on reaching Payagale, the light tanks reported the village held in strength.

Payagale is a long village, about one mile from north to south, but extremely narrow. The houses on the right of the road stretch up to the railway line, which runs parallel with the road and some two hundred yards to the west. The village to the east was at the most only one hundred and fifty yards wide. The houses were very close together, and it was one of the worst villages, from the stand point of village fighting, possible to meet. Almost every house

---

[4] *Fauji Akhbar* was the title of an Indian Army periodical paper printed in English and Hindi.

contained a bunker dug in beneath it, or else a sniper, whilst once again the railway embankment was riddled with small bunkers, most of which contained automatic weapons.

It was verified later that a Japanese Engineer Battalion, numbering some three hundred men, held the position. We were amazed at the time of the attack at the number of booby traps, mines, electric detonations and aerial bombs that were encountered in the village. This made it difficult for tanks to operate with the infantry, and they did so at considerable loss to themselves. In all one squadron had four tanks burn up; one, upon reaching the bridge, blew up on an aerial bomb and completely overturned. The crew crawled out of the tank some ten minutes later in a very badly burned condition.

The attack was identical with the attack on Pyinbongyi, with the exception that A Company attacked on the right of the village, there were no Gurkhas, and C Company took the left flank. 'A' Company boundaries included the road and railway. We again had artillery support and once again the attack was in two phases. The first bound being before the nullah running from east to west through the centre of the village, and the second and final bound a small bund some three hundred yards beyond the southern edge of the village.

The start time for the attack was 9.30 a.m. and it was not until 4 p.m. that we were able to report Payagale clear of the enemy. B Company once again followed behind the other two companies and mopped up the odd few snipers that remained. It was a yard by yard advance and by the time the village had been cleared there was very little left but rubble and smoking ruin.

The action proved very expensive to the Japanese, who lost over two hundred men, but if it was expensive for the enemy it was also one of the most costly for us. Our casualties in this action amounted to 1 officer killed, 1 VCO killed, 9 Indian other ranks killed, and 28 wounded. The officer was Major S.H. Payne MC. His loss to this battalion and indeed to the Indian Army was truly a great one. He had been with the battalion longer than any other officer, and was a great favourite amongst both officers and men. The help he had given to junior officers, who greatly outnumbered the old hands, cannot be measured, except that the deeds of the battalion in action reflect considerably his teaching to all. He was one of the greatest young soldiers in the Indian Army, both during the days when war was only dawning upon India, and later at its zenith.

The battalion harboured with the tanks for the night at MS 63½ , and although we had not made the objective Pegu, after two days, hindsight tells us that it was these two days of hard fighting which caused the fall of the objective with not a great deal of further opposition, except from the centre of the town.

PEGU

We stayed for the next day in our harbour at MS 63½   whilst 63rd Brigade took on Payagi, the next village beyond Payagale. A very heavy divisional artillery strike was put down on Payagi and a considerable call on air support was made. However, the enemy if he had meant to hold the place changed his mind before the troops of 63rd Brigade entered, for they found the place clear.

. So the stage was all set for the attack on Pegu itself. 63rd Brigade were to attack from the north and north-west with, in support, Probyn's Horse, whilst our column was detailed to make a wide flanking movement to the east and capture the Pegu River bridge, near the southern limits of the town. Good reconnaissance would have shown the impossibility of getting tanks in to capture the bridge and yet air-photos did not reveal this complication.

We completed the sweep round with no opposition. Several local people, who said they had just come out from Pegu gave us information which was of little value. Estimates of enemy in Pegu, according to them, varied from 200 to 4,000, although they said that the Japanese would not allow them to know very much, certain areas being out of bounds.

The first tank which went over the bund running from east to west and to the north of the Pegu River, became firmly wedged in a further nullah which took a similar course to the river Pegu. This particular nullah was well covered by automatic crossfire, whilst the country around was thick jungle. We managed to make some headway, but the progress was very slow.

Meanwhile the attack from the north met considerable opposition. It was decided that as the attack from our end was not possible, we should pull out and come round to the north-east of the town, stay the night, and be ready for a possible further move in support the next day.

We went into harbour near Pegu itself, whilst the battle by 63rd Brigade went on furiously, our troops consolidating the part of the town already captured. At night the battle went on spasmodically, but the enemy began pulling out, though not before they had blown the vital bridge. The town was eventually cleared early the next morning, and amongst prisoners taken were some Japanese nurses who later did some very good work for their wounded and prisoners.

The fact that the bridge at Pegu had been destroyed meant some delay for the armour, and some time had to be spent in recce and building a temporary bridge. During the delay the whole battalion stayed in the same camp and the CO decided, owing to depletion of the ranks, upon re-organization. The two Punjabi Musalman (PM) companies were amalgamated and a strong defence platoon (all Musalman) chosen whilst the Hindu Rajputs from the defence platoon were divided between A and C Companies to bring them up to strength, although this still left them far below their war strength establishment.

CHAPTER 6

1945: Hlegu and the Ending

To keep up the momentum of our drive, it was decided that the light tanks, which could make the river crossing more easily, should now carry a company of infantry and push on ahead. Whilst the remainder of the column would follow on at the fastest possible speed.

Our hold up at Pegu, thanks to the fact that our enemy had successfully blown all road bridges going south, meant that the Japanese were able to escape south through the Sittang Valley, so we retraced our steps back to Nyaunglebin in order to turn to the east along a road to Medauk to explore Shwegyn. D Company were now relieved from their SP Gun protection role and given the job of cracking down the road with the light tanks. Captain R.L. Sen was commanding D Company at that time. On 2 May they moved out, whilst the rest of the battalion followed close upon their heels. D Company made very good progress, so much so in fact that it took us some time to catch up and then only when they were brought to a halt owing to another bridge having been blown – this time impassable to any kind of traffic until the sappers had put in two or three days' hard work. The rest of the battalion returned to MS 32½ ..

It was during D Company's sweep towards Shwegyn that sadly a sniper killed Captain R.L. Sen. As it turned out, our last officer casualty of the campaign.

Meanwhile C Company cleared a small village, which had been re-occupied by the Japanese after our forward elements had gone through. It was in this village that we succeeded in capturing two 47 mm guns, in excellent condition although very heavily booby-trapped. These two very excellent trophies now reside at the Rajput Regimental Training Centre in Fatehgarh.

We spent several days at MS 32½ where we joined up with D Company and the Light tanks. D Company related their adventures, for they had met several small parties of Japanese on the way south. With few casualties to themselves they acquitted themselves very well, accounting for something in the neighbourhood of seventy or eighty of the enemy. We lingered for a few days whilst part of 48th Brigade, who waded across the *chaung* and made their way to Hlegu, the last big town before Rangoon.

It is history now that neither 5th, 17th, nor 19th Divisions made Rangoon first, much to the disappointment of 'Punch' Cowan who commanded 17th Division. Every member of his Division equally shared this disappointment, but we had to content ourselves with the knowledge that even if we were not the captors of Rangoon, at least we had had most to do with it, ably supported by the tanks. In the event fate decreed that our leading troops from 48th Brigade, should meet troops of another Indian Division at Hlegu who had made an unopposed landing at Rangoon and found the place unoccupied except for the odd thirty or forty Japanese who had been left behind.

We had plenty to do before the end of May; firstly we had to guard Mingladon airport for the official surrender and then in the middle of the month we had orders to move back to Nyaunglebin and then east to Medauk and thence across the Sittang to Shwegyin.

Shwegyn is perhaps one of the nicest towns in Burma, we certainly had a pleasant aspect, although we undertook a lot of patrol work trying to track down the Japanese who were coming down from the north in their attempt to escape down to Moulmein, on the coast to the east of Rangoon. However, for the time being we had had our main actions, although more were to follow when the

Japanese attempted to escape from the Pegu Yomas in their frantic breakout.

After these actions the Official War Diary quotes:

... and if certain names and groups have been mentioned in this resume, it can hardly be said that they were the only or most deserving within the Battalion. One could mention dozens more for their excellent work, but what mattered was that we were one Unit and, to the best of our knowledge and belief, there was not one man who did not make an excellent job of anything that he was called upon to do and. . . .

This is perhaps a suitable time in the battalion's history to summarize our participation in operation EXTENDED CAPITAL. So brilliantly conceived by General Slim at the outset, though with the benefit of hindsight it has to be acknowledged that with the enemy's slow reaction to our swift advance 'helped' to make the campaign the success it was.

Throughout its engagements the paltan worked in accordance with its teaching and the years of training on the NWF and the 'final polish' in Bethmangla and Ranchi. This all meant that its service was not only sought but highly valued – it had that essential spark which earned it the title the 'Dashing Sixth'.

Further plaudits for the Sixth's professionalism came from our former CO and Lord Wavell.

An extract from a letter written in late 1945 by the battalion's former CO, now Brigadier E.A. Hayes-Newington DSO OBE, and commanding 46th Brigade stated:

The old 6/7th were and are second to none. They fought like hell and seemed quite to enjoy the party. I never met a tired man in my Battalion however stiff the day or fight. I had of course a grand team. I am sorry for all the good friends I have lost.

Everyone did their duty without fail. The battalion's 'War performance' was acknowledged by the late Field Marshal (FM) Lord Wavell when he wrote:

. . . and I have soldiered for more than 42 years and the more I have seen of war the more I realise how it ALL depends on Administration and Transportation and. . . .

And the Sixth had both!

A New Commanding Officer

The monsoon had now started in earnest and our CO, Lieutenant Colonel Hayes-Newington, was promoted to command 99th Brigade east of Meiktila involved in hilly country towards the Shan States. Our new CO arrived in a downpour. Two officers were also there who had been in Quetta in 1942 and remembered only too well that very distinguished Major in a Baluch Mess kit – would he remember us? A frantic search for his name then ensued, which was Lieutenant Colonel B.F. Montgomery MBE. With some unease, we welcomed him. Thankfully, and in his wisdom, Quetta had been left behind, and in the meagre *basha* which served as our Mess, Lieutenant Colonel Montgomery called for a *gin piaz*[1] which put us all at ease.

The battalion was now in a small village about 8 miles to the east of the main Meiktila–Rangoon Road on the end of a branch line coming from Nyaunglebin to Medauk. The road to it was on top of a tortuous bund, muddy and deeply rutted, so the railway had to work. We managed to obtain some railway wheels to convert a jeep and thus, with the help of a long flat car with drop sides, we were able to move the battalion's kit, ammunitions, petrol and essential supplies with comparative ease. We were also fortunate to find a small trolley, which was decked with railway sleepers. This we put in front of the jeep as we felt that this was a safer way of proceeding. The 'break out' of the Japanese was in progress and we did not relish the thought of being knocked out and possibly the driver

---

[1] Gin with a small pickled onion in it.

being killed. Thus the heavy railway truck in front afforded some protection.

All went well until we rounded the bend before our destination, only to find that the points were not set towards the clear track ahead but instead for a siding on which were standing two 30-ton trucks, loaded with raw rubber bales. Signals had been made to the jeep driver to stop, but the weight and momentum of the loaded flat, travelling at approximately 8 mph, was too much for the jeep to hold. Impact became inevitable. As I rolled down the embankment, and off the trolley on which I had been travelling, I was left with two impressions: the look of surprise on Jai Singh's face as he saw me rolling by and the sleepers from the trolley being tossed into the air like matchsticks on impact. The trucks were knocked over and rolled down the embankment, the trolley had been partially buckled, but our long flat and the jeep were intact and we had at last come to a stop! Thereafter bends and points were approached with extreme caution.

Whilst in this small village we had attached to us and under our command two 25-pounders field guns manned by the Royal Artillery. The railway and all the countryside to our west was open country, with paddy fields, and to our east towards the Sittang region it was heavily wooded. Sizeable targets for artillery were not in the offing, though for closer work our 3-inch mortars were made for just this type of countryside.

One day a signal arrived from IV Corps, via 17th Division, to inform us that a Major General Royal Artillery, a 'Master Gunner' no less, would be visiting us; we also discovered that he had come from Italy and was the gunner who had been in charge of the bombardment of Monte Cassino. We were agog to know what target was going to be bombarded and where the concentrations of the many regiments of artillery were, which such a senior gunner would inevitably command. The General arrived with his staff and he was shown the two well cleaned 25-pounders

Plate 17: Nyaunglebin June–July 1945 Monsoon. View of the main road to Rangoon – our medical hut where Lieutenant Sen of the Indian Medical Services (IMS) worked.

Plate 18: On a dry day Lieutenant Colonel Brian Montgomery MBE pins a 'Mention in Dispatches'.

Plate 19: Jawans building a bund to stop our HQ from being undermined by water.

Plate 20: The bridge carried the main road – the mass and force of the monsoon water is well shown here.

and the Lieutenant commanding them. It must have dawned on the General that firstly 14th Army did not possess large numbers of artillery regiments and that the Japanese were not going to supply him with targets like Monte Cassino! To our great relief the 'brass' left us.

However, our position was not ideal to handle a potential Japanese breakout, so we were pulled back to Nyaunglebin to help stem the number of Japanese coming from the Pegu Yomas who would have to cross the river near our position there. Remnants of the Japanese 33rd Army were seeking to re-group but it was quite clear from some of the prisoners we took that their medical services and supplies had completely broken down and that they had not had supplies for at least two months and beri-beri was rife.

It was obvious that we would have to capture Singapore, as the next stage. For this elements of 5th Indian Division were arriving from Rangoon and Operation ZIPPER began to take shape.

Then quite suddenly we heard the news that the first and second atomic bombs had been dropped on Japan itself. The war was over – but would the Japanese military elements still in Burma surrender or would they have to be hunted down? Would elements of the Burma National Army, which had been helping the Japanese during the war, decide for peace or did they have to be fought as well?

Fortuitously the Japanese forces in Burma ceased operations and there was a formal surrender by the Japanese on Mingladon airfield north of Rangoon. Thereafter our battalion was moved across the Sittang to Thaton to take the surrender of the Japanese 33rd Army, about which our Colonel, Brian Montgomery wrote so well and which is reproduced here as Annexure A.

It was our new Colonel's first major move of the battalion, and he was naturally concerned that everything should go like clockwork. I remember assuring the Colonel that the whole battalion was very well versed in moving and that this had been our daily life for the previous six months. He would not hear of it. He was due at Brigade HQ for briefing and asked me to prepare a detailed Movement Order for vehicles, men and materials and the order in which all should move. 'Back to Imphal days', were my thoughts – however, as acting Second-in-Command, I asked the Adjutant and QM to sit down at our makeshift Mess table with paper and pencil and proceed to execute the CO's order. I was being most unfair as neither had been involved at Imphal and I should have known better.

Alas, after our second gin the Colonel returned and demanded to see the Orders for the morrow. There were none and I expected the heavens to fall. The Colonel said nothing, sat down, and called for a sheet of paper and pencil; in ten minutes produced a detailed Movement Order and Load Tables for all vehicles and the order in which they were to move. It was accurate, precise and a tour de force that only a Staff Officer of outstanding ability could have achieved. The Head Clerk was summoned and asked to reproduce the orders for all Company Commanders and the senior subedars.

The Colonel had to leave next morning ahead of us to go directly to Thaton, and a makeshift footbridge across the river Billin had been made safe for his jeep by the engineers. The Subedar Major came to see me about his copy of the Movement Order: would the Colonel mind if certain men and loads were transferred to other lorries? My reply was that we have moved for the past six months practically every day, the Colonel would leave ahead of us, and that it was incumbent on us to get the whole battalion, kit and men to Thaton in one piece without leaving anyone or anything behind. The start time was 6.30 a.m. – any further questions Subedar Major Sahib?

Next morning we saw the Colonel off and the battalion moved off. When, however, we reached the so-called

Plate 21: Japanese Surrender at Mingladon Airfield
August 1945.

The aircraft was painted with large red crosses.
Top right hand corner: one of the escorting Spitfires.

Plate 22: Japanese aircrew of both planes. Most are
wearing silk gloves.

'bridge' over the Billin, which was in spate, the engineers informed us that crossing was not possible as those supports left were not strong enough for the task.

Earlier the bridge had been partially blown up by the retreating Japanese troops and was, in our opinion, 'unsafe'. So we borrowed an amphibious DUKW from the engineers and managed to motor it sufficiently upstream and anchor it to allow us to trail a stout rope from its stern. The end of this was securely fixed to a large pontoon (also borrowed from the engineers), which was capable of carrying our larger vehicles. The idea was to use the current to propel us across the stream, helped by a makeshift pole. Luckily we had found the remnants of a track cut through either side of the nullah so all we had to do was to construct a ramp to allow vehicles to drive onto the pontoon this side and off it on the other side.

It took us from almost nine hours to ferry the whole battalion across, but we succeeded without major catastrophes and finished up arriving in Thaton by five in the evening. I think we were all relieved.

The object in coming to Thaton was to take the surrender of Japanese 33rd Army whose HQ was well outside Thaton to the east. A quick house-to-house search produced a small but well provisioned HQ complete with long range wireless transmitter manned by a Colonel and four Japanese NCO signallers. They were all in good health and at first we were puzzled until we discovered that they were all members of the notorious Kempitai Secret Police! Their formal arrest and search was carried out without delay, all weapons and clothing being removed to prevent suicide and the Military Police notified for their collection. I believe our prompt action helped us greatly in the surrender proceedings as one got the impression that HQ Japanese 33rd Army were glad to have got rid of them!

Whatever their feelings the Japanese army were punctilious in their behaviour, as indeed were we. When we moved subsequently to Paan, across the Salween river, A

Company was left on the west bank to patrol, repair and maintain 34 bridges in their area across which our main access road ran. Fortunately we had a full Japanese Engineer company under command and they would set out every day to check the bridges and repair and maintain as necessary – a task to which they were suited – using local timber and vines as their material. 'A' Company's real task was to patrol an area of about 15 × 60 miles north and south of our road for *dacoits*[2] and escaped Japanese army personnel.

By September the monsoon had all but ceased and the vegetation was extremely lush so most of the patrolling was done on foot; to cover the area adequately we had to take some risks, though all houses and villages were approached with the caution of experienced and battle hardened soldiers.

Whilst at Thaton, and being very under-strength in officers, there appeared one day a very smart and well-groomed officer who introduced himself to the Colonel as Major Guman Singh and informed him that he had been sent as our new Second-in-Command. The Colonel had not received any papers or notice of this important posting and was, to put it mildly, somewhat taken aback at this announcement. It was usual practice for the Colonel to be consulted first by those responsible, to see if he approved of such an appointment! And before the applicant appeared! To add to this, the Colonel had had to deal with a most supercilious member of the new Civil Administration, a Police Superintendent, who coolly informed the CO that he felt that he outranked the Colonel and would be pleased to dine in our Mess! The Colonel was not amused and Mr Edwards, for that was his name, was told to look after himself and that he, Lieutenant Colonel Brian Montgomery was commanding at Thaton and no one else. All in all it had not been the CO's day – so to cool matters

---

[2] Local bandits.

down I gave Major Guman Singh my jeep and asked my driver to take him round our area to acquaint him with the battalion's responsibilities and area.

Once we had dealt with the physical aspect of the surrender in and around Thaton we moved about 20 miles east to the river Salween and crossed it to Paan. 'A' Company[3] and a Japanese Engineer Company were retained on the west bank to patrol for dacoits and any elements of Japanese forces; and the Japanese Engineers to maintain the 34 bridges on the road we had come down on.

The Japanese Engineers mentioned earlier had also in their possession a diesel-engined riverboat, which functioned as a ferry to cross the Salween to Paan and was sometimes used for patrol work, mainly up river. On one such occasion we motored upstream for about five hours to inspect a village on the right bank. On arrival, and because of the awful noise of our engine and the visible presence of a very gnarled Japanese NCO who was the engineer and helmsman, the village appeared empty and devoid of life. We approached after a while and hearing and seeing nothing, I got up and walked into the clearing of the village and called out several times but with no response. We peered into several houses and all appeared to be in order so the villagers had obviously taken flight at our approach, thinking perhaps that we were the Japanese returning.

Suddenly to my right a voice with an unmistakable Cambridge University accent said, 'Why didn't you tell me that you were Indian Army, I expected anything but that!' The words came from a man dressed as a Burman who turned out to be a Karen,[4] and also the head of the village, who had studied law at Cambridge before the war. He insisted that the whole patrol should rest and eat with the

---

[3] A/Maj S.D.M. Ottowell commanded A Company and the M.T. at this point in time.

[4] Karen people live in an area to the east of Burma.

villagers who came out of the surrounding jungle to join us – a very pleasant interlude for us all.

Some may wonder what happened to our boat and the Japanese 'jack of all trades' on board – well, he had his rations and his orders, and his discipline was such that having accepted defeat our orders were accepted and embraced as he had embraced orders from his own superiors before. Thus, whilst the vessel was within sight of us in the village, I had no concern that he would suddenly drift off down river leaving us there.

While digressing on the Japanese soldier and his qualities, there was near our camp opposite Paan the Burmese village of Kuzeik. One day the headman came to see me to complain about the Japanese Engineering Company nearby and in particular one of its soldiers who he said had raped a girl from the village. Obviously I had neither the time, manpower nor resources to investigate this matter and our doctor, Captain Sen, Indian Medical Service (IMS), was a very busy man with the battalion at Paan. So I decided to test the strength of the Japanese Army discipline by summoning the Japanese Engineer Company Commander and asking him to find out and, if successful, punish the culprit in accordance with the procedures of his own forces. The outcome is given in Annexure B. I make no apology for the English, being a direct translation from the Japanese by our interpreter there.

About this time news of the forthcoming elections and independence of India came in the form of directives from GHQ. So on two battalion parades the news was given to all about these forthcoming elections and the move to independence. Many separate company parades were held in order to explain what and who the elections were about and to deal with questions and problems arising. Company Commanders became 'acting unpaid political agents' but sadly the nuts and bolts were temporarily missing because no one was able to spell out the future exactly. At that time Partition was mentioned but not confirmed. Of course no one knew where the Army would stand in future. But with hindsight that Rajput and 'great man' of the Regiment, FM Carriappa, would answer one of the most important questions that most jawans asked, 'who would ensure law and order in the countryside'. FM Carriappa ensured this by keeping the army loyal to the country and not letting it get involved in politics.

But I digress. For the writer, who had been commissioned into the Indian Army and the Rajputs, in particular, I could see no future. The war was over and it was time to leave a service unrivalled anywhere in the world. I had been fortunate and honoured in having fought, lived and eaten with men of the 6th Battalion, the Rajput Regiment, the 'Dashing Sixth'.

After numerous *Khanas*[5] I left in December 1945, taking with me a special Japanese sword for presentation to FM Lord Montgomery of Alamein from the CO (his brother) and All Ranks of the 6th Battalion. My journey to the Tactical HQ in Germany is described briefly in Annexure C.

But to continue with the paltan's life: early in 1946 Lieutenant Colonel M. Raza took over command from Lieutenant Colonel Brian Montgomery, who was posted to the Baluch Regiment from whence he had originated, and the battalion's officers were made up to full strength.

Post hostilities the battalion continued active patrolling throughout the region north of Moulmein and oversaw the final departure to Japan of all Japanese elements still in Burma – thus freeing the country from the presence of its former enemy. Meanwhile the Partition of the Indian subcontinent gradually became a political reality and the battalion was brought back to Fatehgarh to be split in two. All PM personnel went to the Punjab Regiment and sadly, because it was a wartime-raised unit, it was decided that other units in the regiment would absorb

[5] Farewell meals.

Plate 23: Officers of the 6th Battalion prior to Partition at Fatehgarh 1946–7.

Back Row: Lieutenant R.P. Lowry, Mohammed Ilyas and V.D. Kulshrestha, Captains A.D. Nicol and Sardul Singh, Lieutenant D.H. Cloake.

Front Row: Captain D.C.P. Blake, Majors Bhicajee and Ram Singh, Lieutenant Colonel N.A.M. Raza, Major J.E.G. Mills, Captain M.F. Taylor, Anon.

the Hindu Rajput element. Thus the 6th ceased to exist in 1947.

It would seem that all the work, training, experience, many personal disappointments and the final and ultimate sacrifice by all ranks of the paltan, were in vain, 'thrown away'. On the other hand the battalion that had been raised in wartime to help in the emergency, did its duty and completed all tasks to everyone's satisfaction. The emergency finished, the need for this battalion had ceased to exist and what need there was could be absorbed by the regular battalions of the regiment, who had, in fairness, the prior right and honour to continue, their histories going back to John Company days. They were the core of the Regiment.

Subsequently it was my good fortune to meet Lieutenant Colonel (Retired) Mustasad Ahmad, the Colonel who re-raised the 6th Battalion in 1963. We became firm friends. Since its re-raising, the battalion has enjoyed some of the best commanding officers the regiment was able to furnish. Thus it seemed only fitting that during my three visits in 1987, 1992 and again in 2005 to the re-raised 6th Battalion, I found much of the spirit of the old 6/7th pervading in the 6th Battalion (Meiktila) Rajput Regiment, as it was now named; I found them truly worthy successors to the old 6/7th.

Orders for Surrender

From:
Lieutenant Colonel B.F. Montgomery MBE
Commanding British Forces Thaton

To:
The Officer Commanding
Japanese 33 Army.

In accordance with my mandate of authority from the Officer Commanding British Forces Mokpalin – Martaban Area you are responsible to me for compliance with the following order.

1. You will send a Senior Staff Officer to attend at my Headquarters on 3rd October when detailed arrangements for the execution of these orders will be explained to him.
2. This officer will be at the road junction at Taingtaya at 1000 hours where he will be met by a British Officer who will escort him to my Headquarters. He should travel in his own transport.
3. You will establish a permanent contact post at Taingtaya, which will be in telegraphic communication with your Headquarters, and at such other places as I may indicate later.
4. You will detail a Staff Officer as contact Officer with my Headquarters. This Officer will not be changed without my orders. If he does not speak English an interpreter will be necessary in addition.
5. No Japanese Officer or man, either on foot, mounted, or in motor transport, will move beyond the limits of the

concentration areas at present allotted them, without my authority to do so. When such authority is granted they will move always with an escort of the forces under my command.

6. As soon as possible you will submit a strength return, by units in detail including locations, of all Japanese Troops within the area under my Command. This area will be shown on a map to your representative. Three copies of the return will be required which thereafter will be submitted twice weekly.

7. My representatives, including medical officers, will periodically inspect the camps occupied by your troops with special reference to hygiene and sanitary arrangements.

8. You will report when the Field Hospitals, referred in paragraph 6 of the orders issued to you by the Officer Commanding British Forces Mokpalin-Martaban, have completed their movement into their concentration areas.

9. As soon as possible you will report your estimate of the date by which all ration supplies, including reserves, now at your disposal will have been consumed.

10. At a time and place to be notified you will surrender into the keeping of the Forces under my command and all weapons, arms, equipment, and war like stores of all natures in the possession of your troops. The actual arrangements for disarmament will be explained to your representative. See also paragraphs 13–14 below.

11. You will furnish me with a list in detail, by categories, of all items of arms and equipment thus surrendered.

12. You will report to me in writing when all the troops under your command have been completely disarmed.

13. Japanese dumps of arms and ammunition within the area under my command, and referred in paragraph 5 of the orders issued to you by the Officer Commanding British Forces Mokpalin-Martaban, will be handed over to my troops on the ground. The time and date for this will be notified later. In the meantime your guards over these dumps may remain armed.

14. Guards, if any, referred in paragraph 13 of the same instructions, may also remain armed till their duties have been assumed by British Troops. You will inform me of the location and strength of such guards.
15. On completion of disarmament certain working parties will be found by the troops under your command the details of which will be notified to you later.

Lieutenant Colonel

(B.F. MONTGOMERY)

For Brigadier
for Supreme Allied Commander
South East Asia

Issued to: F.H. Khan
Chief of Staff to 33 Army Headquarters
Thaton 2nd October 1945

Statement of
Japanese Commander

(As translated from the Japanese by our interpreter)

To the English Army   at Kuzeik 19th November 1945
Captain Masafuni Nakaya The 1st Company Commander
of the Engineer Regiment.

LANCE CORPORAL GUCHI TAKAHASHI BELONGING
TO THE 1ST COMPANY.

I.   Lance Corporal G. Takahashi has committed the pro-
hibition that every Japanese must not approach to any
of Burmese house. He entered into the village, intend-
ing to gather wild grasses and on his way he stopped at
a Burmese house to light a cigarette.
Captain M. Nakaya sent the Lance Corporal to the
village to gather some kind of wild grasses to be used as
food, because we Japanese lacking of fresh vegetable.

II.   The Colonel's dispositions:
After examined the fact, admonished strictly the Captain
and the Lance Corporal for their misdeeds.
Ordered to all Japanese parties under his Command,
in future they must not approach to a Burmese house
and cannot go out the limitation undermentioned.
Eastward   – the right bank of the Salween River
Southward · – the jetty of Kuzeik
Westward   – 200 yards from the Camping Area
Northward – 200 yards from the Camping Area

(Signed) IKUJI IMASAKA,
Colonel Commander of the Japanese Parties at
Kuzeik & Hlainbwe

Japanese Sword Presentation to Field Marshal Montgomery

Account of the Presentation of the Japanese
Sword to Field Marshal Viscount Montgomery
by the 6th Battalion The Rajput Regiment on
20 January 1946

Arriving in England on repatriation in January 1946, I brought with me a Japanese sword which I was to present on behalf of the Officers and Men of the 6th Battalion to Field Marshal Viscount Montgomery. I was fully aware of the great honour my mission entailed: so with quaking heart I put pen to paper and informed the FM of my arrival. This letter was answered first by the War Office in the form of a telephone call giving me instructions for my journey, and, then by a letter from the FM telling me exactly what to do and where to go. Suggesting that I would like to stay for a few days at his Tac HQ and see a little of Germany!

At 9 o'clock in the morning, on 20 January, I reported to the War Office complete with sword; they shot me off in a car to Hendon aerodrome. On the way we collected Brigadier Belcher, BGS on the FM's staff and arriving at the airport we were greeted by Squadron Leader Duncan who was in charge of the FM's 'Flight'. The aircraft, a shining silver Dakota with the 21st Army Group flash painted on its nose, was standing ready on the tarmac. We climbed aboard and having settled ourselves comfortably in, we took off and with a good tail wind were soon over the Channel. As it was lunchtime a carton was brought to us containing some excellent sandwiches, which to the accompaniment of some lunch hour music over the wireless, were quickly eaten. Our tail wind held good and an hour and fifty minutes from take off we touched down at Osterwalde near Osnabruck. Having thanked Squadron Leader Duncan for the excellent flight, we went to Tac HQ by car. The FM's HQ was situated in a lovely two-winged Schloss surrounded by parkland.

I was met by Captains Chavasse and Henderson, Aide de Camps (ADCs) to the FM who showed me to my room and put me generally at my ease. I gathered that I was now living quite 'en famille' as there was only the FM, his two ADC's, his Personal Assistant and his Military Secretary living within the Schloss.

At teatime the great moment arrived: I was introduced to the FM who, though he had recently been ill, looked quite fit and well. He questioned me a lot about the last campaign in Burma and about the part my battalion took in that show. The FM then suggested that the sword be presented there and then, so that literally I presented the sword over a cup of tea. He then told me that this was only to see what the sword was like and proceeded to inspect it. He ordered the Army photographers and the formal presentation to take place the next day at 2 o'clock.

Tea being over, the FM took me into his study and showed me all his English and foreign decorations. Including the famous Soviet Order of Victory which was studded with diamonds and rubies; and no less brilliant were the various township gifts which had been presented to the FM on his receipt of their freedoms. Then it was my turn and I was presented with the book the FM had written himself, entitled *From El Alamein to the River Sangro*, to which he added his best wishes and autograph. It was then time for dinner and having been thoroughly dazzled by the brilliant spectacle of gold cups and the Danish Order of the Elephant, I went to join his ADCs for a quick drink before dinner. This was excellent and the FM a perfect host. And so ended the first day.

The next day's programme was all mapped out by the FM

himself and, weather permitting, I was to be shown Osnabruck, Cologne and the Rhine Valley from the air to see how effective Bomber Command had done its work. At 2 o'clock the formal presentation was to take place, after which it was suggested that I would like to go and see Osnabruck by car. As it happened, the next morning's weather did not permit any flying so Captain Chevasse showed me Osnabruck, which in sections, and particularly the marshalling yards, had been completely razed to the ground. The destruction had been systematic and complete and did not leave a wall standing. We arrived back at Tac HQ in time for lunch. Air Chief Marshal, Sir Sholto Douglas, arrived later and joined us for dinner with the FM.

At 2 o'clock I was ready with the sword and the FM dressed in battledress wearing the famous two-badge beret, came into the room. I then presented the sword in the name of the officers and men of the 6th Battalion The Rajput Regiment. The FM thanked the Battalion very much and said that he would have a silver plate made with a suitable inscription hung just above the sword. In the meantime, the photographer was busy taking his shots. The FM was delighted with the present, admiring the keen blade and wrought iron hilt on which, among other decorations there were three nasty looking Japanese faces carved in relief.

The presentation over, Captain Henderson and I explored the surrounding countryside on horseback, my companion riding Rommel's famous charger which I was informed had been brought out of captivity from Denmark. Tea and Dinner followed much too soon and having discussed at great length the FM's proposed visit to Switzerland, we went to bed.

The next morning after a hearty breakfast, my departure was fixed, the weather permitting me to fly. Before wishing my old Battalion and me God speed and the very best of luck, the FM arranged for the plane to fly over Osnabruck and Wesel for me to see Bomber Command's work from the air, as due to the weather I had been unable to see it the day before. At half-past nine I boarded the same Dakota which had brought me out and we were soon off and over

Plate 24: Captain S.D.M. Ottowell with Field Marshal Viscount
Montgomery and the sword.

Osnabruck, though unfortunately low-flying clouds prevent-
ed me from seeing anything of this past target of our bombers.
At Wesel the visibility was good, though what had been a
town was a pile of rubble and fields, with the remnants of a
broken bridge sticking out of the waters of the Rhine. And
so at 12 o'clock I landed at Gatwick Airport.

A great honour had been conferred on an outstanding
battalion by a great man of whom it will always be justly
proud.

ANNEXURE D

Transport: An Explanation

Our establishment consisted of:

1 Officer
1 Havildar
1 L/Naik Clerk
1 Fitter IEME
1 Sepoy and
20 Drivers

From its raising in 1940 to August 1942 I have pieced together the battalion's life from the spoken word of former officers and letters and from the evidence I myself experienced at first hand. Inevitably my interest from 1943 onwards was transport, both mule and motor vehicles, with carriers thrown in. Because as a battalion on the NWF we all relied heavily on transport, both four-legged and wheeled, I became involved in all our activities and thus was aware of the broad battalion picture – in some cases more than the company commanders were. Our excellent cadre of drivers always reported to me if they went out singly on a company job and thus within reason I knew where the vehicle was and afterwards what, if anything, had happened. After all, our lorries were not plentiful, and were worth their weight in gold to us. We could not afford to lose a single one through breakdown or accident; equally obvious; if there was a breakdown 'out in the sticks' Jai Singh and I would have to collect it; so its location, even approximate, was vital. On such very few occasions I informed the Adjutant or CO what I was doing and then the rest was up to me.

I rarely sent Havildar Shah Mohamed out on such an errand because good and speedy recovery was vital and if there were any other vehicles in the vicinity from other units I was, because of rank, in better position to seek the active help from other units, whoever they were. Also we did not waste time with specialists such as the Light Aid Detachment coming to help us, because this usually meant that the 'casualty' would be taken to their base, which never seemed to coincide with ours – and we would be without a vehicle when, for instance, our total vehicle strength was only five 3-tonners and two 15-cwt, such as at Damdil in the beginning. It was imperative that all our vehicles were present and ready at all times.

This may well lead the reader to wonder why there was a need for a MT Section commanded by an officer. It was wartime and our role in the scheme of things could alter in a day. In Peshawar we had seventeen 3-tonners for the MT Section on hire from a civilian contractor, in addition there were a 10 hp Hillman Minx, a Plymouth convertible for the CO, and two staff cars. On paper these were the contractor's sole responsibility for maintenance. This and petrol requisitioning had all to be countersigned by an officer, in addition to which the unit was responsible for providing drivers.

In Damdil we had army vehicles that were our entire responsibility plus four Ford four-wheel-drive carriers and one 250 cc BSA motorcycle. We took all these to Razmak only to exchange our wheeled carriers for tracked Brengun carriers. All of these were then left behind when we went to Bethmangla for jungle training; there we received fifteen brand new 15-cwt army vehicles and two jeeps. These were left behind when we went out to Ranchi to join 17th Division. On arrival with 17th Division we received on loan, so to speak, some twelve 3-tonners and two new jeeps, which we kept.

From the above list the reader will understand that our 'active' driver availability was never more than about twenty-four. Clearly some of the older drivers left us to rejoin their rifle companies for promotion or other reasons, so that over the years we probably had some 48–50 drivers which the battalion had trained.

You may thus imagine our surprise and shock when we were ordered to take 87 assorted vehicles, all declared 'unserviceable' and in army terminology 'third lined'. A total of fifteen 15-cwt plus 87 vehicles meant we had to find 102 drivers at least! And we had four days in which to do it, to say nothing of making 87 assorted vehicles, that had been throughout the north African and Kabaw Valley campaigns, capable of being driven over mountainous dirt tracks to our start line at Palel and of course beyond, to serve us in our dash to Meiktila and subsequently endure to Rangoon.

Thus I found myself, as MTO, at the centre of the battalion's daily work. Before crossing the Irrawaddy River the fighting arm of each motorized battalion was split into A Echelon and B Echelon. The former consisted of twenty four 4 × 4 15-cwt trucks and twelve 30-cwt Dodge trucks with no superstructures (these had all been lost in their previous 'incarnation' in the western Desert but their engines worked and were powerful – our best find from the Plain of Imphal!) We must not forget our one and only 15-cwt water tank vehicle. This Echelon carried those troops not riding on tanks, ammunition, some reserve petrol, the mortar and heavy machine gun platoons. Air supply drops were laid on between the bridgehead, Pagan area and Meiktila airfield which was one of our first tasks to secure, so that supplies could be flown in by Dakota. On flying back to base the Dakotas would take all our wounded. A very simple but effective system.

On this subject and throughout our campaign our doctor, Lieutenant (Later Captain) Sen, Indian Medical Service (IMS), was a tower of strength. All his work was done in the field, either on his jeep or beside it and without regard for his own safety – a very dedicated man, as were his two medical orderlies – both ex-buglers.

Battle Casualties
6th Battalion: The 7th Rajput Regiment

1939–1944

KILLED IN ACTION

OFFICERS	5
VCOs	4
IORs	88

DIED OF WOUNDS

IORs	20

WOUNDED IN ACTION

OFFICERS	2
VCOs	4
IORs	203

Roll of Honour
6th Battalion: The 7th Rajput Regiment

1939–1945

OFFICERS - 5
Major G.R. Marriott
Major J.R. Cox
Major S.H. Payne M.C.
Captain R.L. Sen
Major K. Crossley

VCOs - 4
Jemadar Rang Khan
Jemadar Rehmat Ali
Jemadar Ram Singh
Subedar Shambhu Singh

IORs - 88

13152	Naik	Amir Din
17081	Sepoy	Allah Ditta
28217	Sepoy	Atta Mohd
22711	Naik	Abdul Karim
15530	L/Naik	Abdul Aziz
24816	Sepoy	Ali Sher
11373	L/Havildar	Ahmed Khan
10661	Naik	Ahmed Khan
23884	Sepoy	Bishun Singh
23632	Sepoy	Barmeshwar Nath Singh
24013	Sepoy	Bachan Singh
39196	Sepoy	Bhatai Rai
17173	Sepoy	Bhog Raj Singh

27691	Sepoy	Bhurn
31716	Sepoy	Bishu Nath Singh
35088	Sepoy	Chakar Par Singh
22199	Sepoy	Chander Pal Singh
17145	L/Naik	Fazal Ahmed
16829	Sepoy	Ghulam Mohd
30658	Sepoy	Hakim Singh
25200	Sepoy	Har Phul Singh
15181	L/Havildar	Har Baksh Singh
17195	Sepoy	Heman Chal Singh
15743	Sepoy	Hakim Ali
30277	Sepoy	Hotam Singh
19051	Sepoy	Inayat
31159	Sepoy	Jhuma Khan
31564	Sepoy	Kamala Singh
15855	Naik	Khan Mohd
13442	Sepoy	Lakhpat Singh
23172	Sepoy	Lachhman Singh
13464	Sepoy	Lal Khan
38006	Sepoy	Lal Bihari Singh
14348	L/Naik	Mulaim Singh
26864	Sepoy	Mahabir Singh
21064	Sepoy	Mohd Sharif
17117	Sepoy	Mahilal Singh
40696	Sepoy	Man Singh
16768	Naik	Mahipal Singh
23794	Sepoy	Munshi Singh
33689	Sepoy	Mohd Shafi
18964	Sepoy	Nazar Ali
30843	Sepoy	Malkhan Singh
30779	Sepoy	Nanney Singh
11394	Havildar	Nazir Ahmed
41432	Sepoy	Nasir-ud-din
18660	Sepoy	Nazar Hussain
23262	Sepoy	Nur Mohd
23790	Sepoy	Pahlad Singh
17042	Sepoy	Raghubir Singh
23937	Sepoy	Ram Lakhan Singh
14276	Sepoy	Ram Singh

40498	Sepoy	Ram Naresh Singh
15879	L/Naik	Rehmat Ali
41851	Sepoy	Ram Lachhman Singh
17253	Sepoy	Ram Raj Singh
37872	Sepoy	Sheo Nath
25493	Sepoy	Sita Ram Singh
1199	Havildar	Shiv Nayak Singh
22982	Sepoy	Sunder Singh
27167	Sepoy	Shyam Singh
20361	Sepoy	Sher Mohd
13505	Naik	Shah Mohd
14743	Sepoy	Tilak Singh
26843	Sepoy	Tippan Singh
21123	L/Naik	Umar Din
20031	Sepoy	Umar Din
17247	L/Naik	Vishwa Nath Singh
25075	Sepoy	Badri Singh
31081	Sepoy	Bakhtawar Singh
13976	L/Naik	Bute Khan
27009	Sepoy	Chhattar Singh
40787	Sepoy	Chand Suraj
16953	L/Havildar	Chander Pal Singh
13127	Sepoy	Dhan Singh
34738	Sepoy	Fateh Singh
29212	Sepoy	Hakim Singh
27049	Sepoy	Jodha Singh
24246	Sepoy	Mahender Singh
12909	Havildar	Mohd Akbar
22248	L/Naik	Mohd Ummar
32913	Sepoy	Mohd Ismail
18951	Sepoy	Mohd Hussain
11823	Havildar	Ram Autar Singh
22143	Sepoy	Room Singh
28507	Sepoy	Sardar Singh
17104	Sepoy	Sikandar Khan
42730	Sepoy	Sher Jang

ANNEXURE G

Farewell Letter from Chief of Staff of Japanese 33rd Army

33 Army HQ
Zemathwe, 18 January 1946

Dear Colonel Montgomery,

At this time, our 33rd Army has been ordered to evacuate our present site, and move in the direction of Moulmein, thus leaving your command.

During the encampment of our Army under your command we were able to enjoy a far more wholesome and profitable existence than the one we expect, far exceeding our maximum wishes. I wish to thank you on behalf of the entire Army for your unbiased and sympathetic treatment, which made this possible.

Now at this very time when they are about to step off on their first leg Eastward; the hearts of all the men are throbbing with excitement at the expectancy of being able to see Home. At the same time the officers of the 33rd Army Staff, who have come into contact with you, have all expressed a most unexplainable feeling of not wanting to part from you, which surprises me very much.

In continuing, I would like to express the thankfulness of our Army by some token. However, being that under the present limited conditions, such a thing cannot be done, let me at this time state that if there is anything in the way of handcraft work, you would like to have our men make, please do inform our Staff Officer, Major Fuchi.

Before letting my brush be, I would like to wish you continued good health, and to pray for your future successes.

In closing, I remain

Yours most sincerely,
Major General Rekichiro Sawamoto,
Chief of Staff, 33 Army.

Decorations and Awards
6th Battalion: The 7th Rajput Regiment

MC
SUBEDAR MOHAMMED AFSAR KHAN
SUBEDAR CHUNNI SINGH
MAJOR S.H. PAYNE
JEMADAR MALDEO SINGH

MM
13070 HAVILDAR RAMDEO SINGH
17418 L/NAIK ALI MOHAMMED
14708 HAVILDAR SAHDEO SINGH
17943 L/NAIK MOHAMMED AFSAR
17735 L/NAIK KHAWAT DIN
10607 HAVILDAR BALWANT SINGH
10145 NAIK MOHAMMED KHAN
24923 SEPOY THAKUR SINGH
27049 SEPOY JODHA SINGH
17609 L/NAIK RAGHUBIR SINGH
34734 SEPOY DAL SINGH

DSO
LIEUTENANT COLONEL
    E.A. HAYES-NEWINGTON OBE

Mentioned in Despatches
LIEUTENANT COLONEL
    E.A. HAYES-NEWINGTON DSO OBE
18083 L/NAIK BHAGOTI SINGH
15841 L/NAIK DIP SINGH
16883 L/NAIK JAHAN DAD
21106 L/NAIK KAMPTA SINGH
24923 SEPOY THAKUR SINGH

Indian Distinguished Service Medal
17125 NAIK RAJA KHAN

Certificates of Gallantry
33204 SEPOY GANESH SINGH
320 SWEEPER MAHA

Bibliography

Indian Army Association Newsletters.

Berridge P.S.A., *Couplings to the Khyber*, David & Charles Newton Abbot, 1969.

Perrett Bryan, *Tank Tracks to Rangoon: The Story of British Armour in Burma*, London: Robert Hale, 1978.

6/7th Battalion: The Rajput Regiment *War Diary* by kind permission of Mrs Pat Sheridan (Daughter of Lt. Col. Hayes-Newington).

Ahmad Mustasad, *Heritage: The History of The Rajput Regiment 1778–1947*, New Delhi: Rakesh Press.

Roll of Honour – The Rajput Regimental Magazine, vol. 16, July 1946 produced by the Regimental Centre.

Index